HA

C000293742

BIRT

A COMEDY

MARC CAMOLETTI

Adapted by

BEVERLEY CROSS

SAMUEL   FRENCH

LONDON

NEW YORK   TORONTO   SYDNEY   HOLLYWOOD

ISBN 978 0 573 11172 3

Please see page iv for further copyright information

HAPPY BIRTHDAY

First presented by John Gale at the Apollo Theatre,
London, on the 18th April 1979 with the following cast
of characters:

Jacqueline	Elizabeth Counsell
Robert	Ian Lavender
Bernard	Christopher Timothy
Brigit 1	Julia Foster
Brigit 2	Malou Cartwright

The play directed by Roger Redfarn
Setting by Peter Rice

The action takes place in the living-room of a house in
the country

ACT I   Early evening
ACT II   After dinner, the same night

Time—the present

COPYRIGHT INFORMATION

ACT I

The living-room of a comfortable house in the country. Early evening

The front door, kitchen, bathroom and three bedrooms all open directly into the room. (See plan of set on p. 71)

When the CURTAIN *rises the room is empty. Mozart is playing softly from the record-player. After a moment the phone starts to ring. Jacqueline enters from the bathroom, a hairbrush in her hand, and goes to answer the telephone, which is by the fireplace*

Jacqueline Hello? . . . Yes, this is she. . . . Yes. That's right. . . . Who? . . . Ah, the agency—you've managed to find someone? . . . Marvellous! . . . Not quite a housekeeper, and not quite a charwoman? . . . Something between the two? . . . A temporary? . . . Well, never mind. My husband and I are expecting a guest for the week-end. Can she come today? . . . Wonderful! . . . Later—and the money is agreed. Fine. And what's her name? . . . Brigit? That's very suitable. . . . Sweet. Thank you very much, I'm terribly grateful. Good-bye.

Jacqueline replaces the telephone and exits to the bathroom

There is a ring at the front doorbell

Jacqueline enters, switches off the music, and opens the door. Robert stands there with a suitcase and a bunch of roses, and wearing a hat

Robert It's me. I've arrived.

Jacqueline pulls him inside, kicks the door shut behind him, and kisses him

Where is he?
Jacqueline Down below, in the cellar.
Robert Good.

She tries to kiss him again

Hold it! Just a minute. What if he decides to come up?
Jacqueline Not possible—he's only just gone down. I just can't believe you're here. It's marvellous. Sheer bliss. Why don't you put your case down? How do you feel?
Robert What?
Jacqueline Is it bliss for you too?
Robert Certainly. If it wasn't bliss I wouldn't be here, would I? I mean, it's terribly dangerous. We must be mad.
Jacqueline Not at all. I tell you, when he told me that he'd invited you down here I could hardly speak I was so excited, so happy. I kissed him for sheer joy—you know what I mean?
Robert Of course. I nearly kissed him too . . .

Jacqueline I kept wanting to ask him to invite you but I didn't dare. Maybe he read my mind—I was completely knocked sideways when he thought up the invitation all on his own.

Robert Well, he was very determined I should come. Insisted on it. Not that I objected that much.

Jacqueline I didn't object at all.

Robert No, you kissed him. He doesn't suspect anything, does he?

Jacqueline Not a thing. He happens to like you very much.

Robert Not quite in the same way as you do.

Jacqueline I hope not.

Robert I'm his oldest friend.

Jacqueline Now don't start getting broody and guilty already–the main thing is that you're here. I was praying that I'd be here alone when you arrived.

Robert That's very touching. But look, we must be very careful. Let's not do anything stupid.

Jacqueline No.

Robert In our situation, even the simplest teeniest thing could give us away. A glance, a touch of the hand . . .

Jacqueline Don't fret, I'll be as careful as a mouse. Would you like to get rid of that case?

Robert Yes. For you. (*He hands her the flowers*)

A door slams off in the kitchen. Robert jumps away, retaining the flowers

Jacqueline Ah! Now then. Here we go. The man himself . . .

Robert Already?

Bernard enters from the kitchen

Bernard Robert, old chap, you're here!

Robert Yes, yes, I've arrived. Just arrived. Arrived a second ago. Just got here.

Jacqueline Yes. A moment ago. You can see that—he's still got his hat on. (*She takes his hat off*)

Robert I'm so sorry.

Bernard That's all right. You make yourself at home. You do just as you like, old chap. It's marvellous to see you, isn't it, darling?

Jacqueline Bliss.

Robert Marvellous to see you too—both of you.

Bernard You're looking very well.

Robert So are you—both of you.

Bernard Thank you.

Robert Not at all. It's splendid, absolutely splendid—and so nice to see both of you again and looking so well on it. I can't thank you enough for inviting me here.

Bernard Oh, come on! An old friend like you. (*To Jacqueline*) If only you knew him as well as I do.

Jacqueline Yes? . . .

Bernard I mean, underneath that shy façade he's really a very extraordinary fellow. (*He boxes Robert playfully on the shoulder*)

Jacqueline Yes, darling, so you've said before . . .
Robert I was only hoping that I wouldn't be putting you out.
Bernard Putting us out? Are you joking, or digging for compliments?
Robert Not at all.
Bernard Then there's nothing to discuss. We are enchanted to see you, aren't we, darling?
Jacqueline Of course.
Robert Me too—enchanted.
Bernard Then that's all right then, so we're all happy. All lovely. So what more could any of us want?
Jacqueline I'd like a glass of champagne.
Bernard And so you shall. Whenever you like.
Jacqueline One thing we mustn't forget—someone must go to the village because everything will be shut there tomorrow.
Bernard No. And another thing—I don't think it's absolutely vital to use the little glasses, do you?
Jacqueline Then we'll use the big ones, all right?
Bernard Absolutely all right.
Jacqueline Absolutely!
Robert Just a minute—what are we talking about? I'm somewhat confused.
Jacqueline Glasses—for the champagne.
Bernard Let's live a little—after all it's the first time you've ever been here.
Robert I'm overwhelmed—so pretty and everything arranged with such a flair. Perfectly charming.
Bernard Praise Jacqueline—she did it all.
Robert Oh, I can see that. Certainly. One only has to look about one. Quite perfect.
Jacqueline I'm delighted it pleases you, but really I don't deserve——
Bernard Of course you do. Have you shown Robert his room?
Jacqueline I was just about to before you came in.
Bernard Fine. Then it's through there—or through there. (*He points in turn to the bedroom down* L *and up* L) You can have whichever one you like.

Jacqueline signals to Robert to take the bedroom down L

Robert Well, how about that one? (*He points down* L)
Bernard You couldn't have chosen better. Make yourself at home.
Jacqueline I'm sure you'd like to unpack your things and all that.
Robert Well, yes—that would be very nice.
Bernard And when you've done all that, if you find it too small or too cluttered, we can always shift you somewhere else.
Robert I wouldn't dream of it. I'm sure it's just fine.

Jacqueline puts Robert's hat on his head

Robert gives her the roses and exits down L

Jacqueline (*closing the door*) The agency called. We're in luck—they're sending us a temporary. Let's hope she's competent.

Bernard Let's hope she's better than the last one.

Jacqueline I didn't choose her. (*She gets a vase from the fire and takes it to the table*)

Bernard No-one in their right mind would have chosen her. Broke all the china and her cooking nearly poisoned me. And ugly into the bargain.

Jacqueline (*arranging the roses loosely*) Ugly? Funny—I thought she looked like your mother... Anyway, she'll be here in an hour. She's called Brigit.

Bernard Brigit? Why is she called Brigit?

Jacqueline I don't know. What's wrong with Brigit?

Bernard Nothing I suppose. It's an unusual name.

Jacqueline Rubbish. I know lots of Brigits.

Bernard Do you?

Jacqueline Of course I do. I had an aunt Brigit, she was a very nice person.

Robert enters

Robert What an attractive room.

Jacqueline You'll be all right in there?

Robert As right side up as a billiard ball. This really is a very lovely house.

Jacqueline Yes, I only wish we were able to spend more time here. And if only living in the country was less complicated—I must finish that list for the village shop. Would you excuse me?

Robert Of course.

Bernard Make sure you get everything down.

Jacqueline I will. I won't be long.

Bernard Take your time, darling.

Jacqueline All right, darling.

Jacqueline exits to the kitchen with the vase and roses

Bernard Take a seat, old boy. And how about a drink?

Robert (*sitting*) Yes, that would be very nice——

Bernard Scotch?

Robert Very nice. Thank you—but no ice.

Bernard starts to mix and pour drinks

Bernard It really is good to see you, Robert, old chap. Marvellous

Robert Just how I feel, Bernard. Wonderful.

Bernard I'm glad you think like that because I really need your help, old man. (*He goes to Robert with two drinks and gives him one*)

Robert My help? Whatever for?

Bernard (*confidentially*) I'll tell you. Listen. We've known each other a long time, haven't we?

Robert A long time. Let me see, it was . . .

Bernard It doesn't matter about *how* long. The point is, over the years, we've seen a lot of each other.

Robert A great deal. But I'm not sure that I quite understand . . .

Bernard Please. I'm being serious—desperately serious. This is what friendship is all about. I have something to tell you—but strictly between you and me. A confidence. A secret. I can rely on you?

Robert I think so. I hope so. Depends what it is.

Bernard I want you to swear, cross your heart, all that sort of thing.

Robert Scout's honour?

Bernard Don't be flippant. This is frightfully important.

Robert Sorry.

Bernard That's all right. I just want to impress on you the need for absolute secrecy.

Robert All right. I'll swear—on what do you want me to swear?

Bernard Your word of honour. As a gentleman.

Robert Very well.

Bernard Well, it's like this—I haven't behaved like a gentleman.

Robert Ah! . . . Good.

Bernard Why do you say "Ah! Good"?

Robert I don't know why. Nerves, I suppose. I just happened to say "Ah! . . . Good." I don't know why I said "Ah! . . . Good." It's just one of those things that happen.

Bernard All right. But you see, old chap, I've got myself into this situation with this—this girl.

Robert Ah! . . . Good.

Bernard You're doing it again.

Robert Am I?

Bernard I'm the one who should be nervous.

Robert Sorry.

Bernard But this situation, this complicated situation is the reason I've asked you to come here—because I *need* you.

Robert Ah! . . . Good.

Bernard Please don't keep saying "Ah! . . . Good."

Robert Sorry—my nerves. And I'm very confused. This situation of yours and all that. I mean, what is it to do with me?

Bernard Simple.

Robert Is it?

Bernard Very simple. I just couldn't think up an excuse, a story to tell Jacqueline. You see, I invited her here so that I can be with her. It's her birthday, you see.

Robert She didn't tell me it was her birthday.

Bernard Who didn't?

Robert Jacqueline didn't.

Bernard Not Jacqueline's birthday—Brigit's birthday.

Robert Who's Brigit?

Bernard That's her name.

Robert Whose name?

Bernard The name of my—well, her name. The name of . . . Let's just say it's her name.

Robert Ah! . . . Good. Yes. Yes. Yes. Brigit. But what's it got to do with me?

Bernard Isn't it clear?

Robert No. Not very.

Bernard I've invited you so that she could come too.

Robert Come too? Here?

Bernard Exactly.

Robert But you're stark raving mad. Come here? Actually invite your mistress to come here?

Bernard No, not at all. Not a bit like that. It's you who've invited her here.

Robert I've never even met her.

Bernard Look, I couldn't invite Brigit myself because Jacqueline knows nothing at all about Brigit. I couldn't just invite a girl down here because it's her birthday. Jacqueline's no fool.

Robert No.

Bernard She'd know something fishy was going on. She'd guess. That's why you've invited Brigit down.

Robert Why?

Bernard Because she's *your* mistress.

Robert What!

Bernard Yes. Your mistress.

Robert (*rising*) Oh, no. No. Oh, no, no, no, no.

Bernard Why not? (*He rises*)

Robert Because—because it's just not on. No, no. None of that. No, no.

Bernard Why not?

Robert Because—because it would never work, that's what.

Bernard Of course it will. It'll work very well.

Robert Never. There's no way.

Bernard Why not?

Robert Why not? Why not? Think about it. Right here in front of your wife; in front of Jacqueline? It can't be done. I mean, what about me? What sort of position would I be in?

Bernard No skin off your nose at all. You're a bachelor. Perfectly in order for you to have a mistress. And what could be more normal than for you to want to bring her down here?

Robert Oh, nothing wrong at all. Except for the fact that I haven't got a mistress.

Bernard That's got nothing to do with it. The point is nobody knows anything at all about your private life. That side of your personality is as much a mystery to me as it is to Jacqueline. She'll think it perfectly ordinary and natural that you should have a mistress. She won't be in the least surprised.

Robert I'm not so sure. But anyway, I don't like it. It's just not my line. I'm just not that sort of chap. I don't want to do it.

Bernard Don't want to? But it's too late not to want to.

Robert What do you mean, too late?

Bernard I've worked it all out with Brigit. (*He goes and pours himself a drink*) It's all agreed. When she gets here, she's going to behave exactly as if she was your girl-friend.

Robert She can do what she likes. But don't count on me to go along with it. I'm not going to be an accomplice to your deceiving your wife. It's just not on, old man. Anyway, she'll see through it like a flash. It just won't work. (*He finishes his drink and puts his glass on the fireplace*)

Bernard Why not?

Robert Why not? Why not? Why do you keep saying "why not" all the time? Just stop it, will you. It's very irritating.

Bernard I repeat myself because I am totally baffled as to why you should refuse to render me this small service.

Robert Because it's impossible.

Bernard Why?

Robert Please, enough of the "whys", "why nots", and "whyever nots". Use your brains for a moment. It just can't possibly work.

Bernard It'll work like a charm.

Robert No——

Bernard Why ever not?

Robert Because nothing rings true—if I *had* a mistress, then it stands to reason we would have arrived together; at the same time.

Bernard Not necessarily. I told her to take the train so that you would get here before her, so that I'd have time to put you in the picture. I've worked it all out very carefully.

Robert I came by car.

Bernard I know you did. What's that got to do with it?

Robert Suppose I'd had an accident?

Bernard But you didn't. Here you are . . .

Robert Not for long . . .

Bernard Why not?

Robert Because I'm not going to stay.

Bernard Why not?

Robert Look, do you mind. I'm up to here with your "whys" and "why nots". It's getting to be a habit with you—a mania.

Bernard Now keep calm, old man. No need to get in a paddy.

Robert I'm not in a paddy. But if you like I'll tell you why—why I'm not going to stay. It's because of this fellow in town. A client—just remembered, frightfully important—can't think how I came to forget him . . .

Bernard What's wrong with him?

Robert Nothing to do with you. You're in insurance—what do you know about escalators?

Bernard Nothing at all.

Robert Then there's nothing to discuss.

Bernard I don't agree. I've always been fascinated by escalators. Tell me about your client.

Robert His escalator won't work.

Bernard Oh! Why not?

Robert Technical reasons. That's why I've got to go back to town in double quick time. Poor chap up there on the third floor can't get down.

Bernard Why doesn't he use the lift?

Robert That doesn't work either.

Bernard Why not?

Robert I've had enough. Where's my suitcase?

Robert exits to the bedroom down L

Bernard You can't do this to me. And even if you do go, I'm still going to have to tell Jacqueline about you and Brigit.

Robert enters, wearing his hat, with his case

Robert I've never even met the wretched woman!

Bernard Now's your chance. I mean, put yourself in my shoes, old man. I'm not going to tell my wife that Brigit's *my* girl-friend, am I?

Robert That's your problem. You tell her what you like. It's nothing to do with me. But I insist you don't involve me. You can't go telling her she's my mistress when I'm not going to be here. No tales behind my back . . . It wouldn't be right.

Bernard Whether you're here or up your escalator, I'm not going to change my story now.

Robert You'll have to—I refuse to have anything to do with such a sordid and complicated tissue of lies—and if you say "why not", so help me, I'll punch you right on the nose!

Jacqueline enters from the kitchen with the roses properly arranged

Jacqueline (*putting the vase on the table*) My darlings! We simply don't have anything! Isn't it frightful living in a house when you don't actually live there all the time—if you know what I mean. You always think everything's there, and when you arrive for the week-end it isn't there at all.

Robert Well, you don't have to trouble on my account, because I'm going.

Jacqueline Going? What do you mean, going?

Bernard Yes, I can't think what's come over him, but he absolutely insists . . .

Jacqueline But whatever for?

Robert I've just explained it all to Bernard. There's this client of mine in town. I'd forgotten all about him. Absolutely essential that I return at once, otherwise he won't get down till Monday.

Jacqueline It's ridiculous.

Bernard That's just what I've been saying.

Jacqueline But, Robert dear, we were so looking forward to having you here. (*To Bernard*) Have you say anything to upset him?

Bernard Only "why not".

Jacqueline What?

Robert Please stop. Never mind . . .

Jacqueline But I do mind. Terribly. Please, for me—forget your client and stay.

Robert Absolutely impossible.

Jacqueline But everything's ready. I've planned a marvellous little dinner —just for the three of us.

Bernard For four.

Jacqueline For three—but there's certainly enough to eat if you men want to eat for four.

Robert No , . .

Bernard Nothing to worry about. Jacqueline's made a list . . .
Jacqueline You're not on a diet, or anything like that, are you?
Robert No.
Bernard There you are, then.
Robert Not at all. There's really no point in going on and on, because I'm leaving.
Bernard It's not going to make any difference, you know.
Jacqueline What on earth are you two talking about?
Bernard Oh, it's just that Robert is so old-fashioned . . .
Robert I'm not old-fashioned.
Bernard Of course you are. So silly in this day and age . . .
Robert Where's my hat? (*He goes to the hat stand looking for his hat*)
Bernard There you are, you see. Can't go without his hat. Old-fashioned. And as shy as a schoolboy. (*To Jacqueline*) You see, what did I tell you?
Jacqueline You haven't told me anything. One moment he's here for the week-end, next moment he wants to go. You say he's old-fashioned and shy—why is he suddenly shy? He's never been shy before.
Robert I'm not shy . . . (*He goes to the fire, still looking for his hat*)
Bernard Of course you are. Just because you've had to confess the truth about your private life—your intimate life.
Jacqueline What intimate life?
Robert Don't listen to him.
Bernard He's told me all about this—this liaison.
Jacqueline What liaison?
Robert I forbid you to listen, Jacqueline.
Bernard You see—just look at him! A bundle of nerves! Can't bring himself to speak of it in front of you . . .
Robert But I never said anything . . .
Bernard It's too late denying it now. If you wanted to keep it all a secret you shouldn't have said anything. Not that it's any business of mine. Your private life is your private life. That you've got a mistress is nothing to do with me.
Jacqueline A mistress!
Robert No, no . . .
Bernard You see, darling—he just can't bring himself to say anything in front of you. It's ludicrous—I mean, why make a drama out of it? We weren't born yesterday. We know all about the way we live now, don't we?
Jacqueline I don't know. I suppose—that's to say . . .
Bernard Of course we do. Come on Robert don't be coy. Just tell her what you told me a moment ago.
Robert I told you nothing.
Bernard Yes you did—all about your girl-friend.
Jacqueline My God . . .
Bernard He's got a girl-friend.
Jacqueline He told you that?
Bernard Just before you came in—what was her name? Bertha? Bernadette? Brenda?

Robert Brigit.

Bernard Ah! You see! That's it, that's the name, Brigit.

Jacqueline Who's Brigit?

Bernard His mistress.

Jacqueline His what? (*To Robert*) It's not true!

Bernard Certainly it's true. He told me all about her—I can't understand why he can't bring himself to tell you all about her.

Jacqueline I don't believe a word of it.

Bernard Why not?

Jacqueline Because—well, I don't know why not. I don't understand why he should tell you and not want to tell me.

Bernard That's what I mean . . .

Jacqueline It's not right. It's despicable. It's the action of a cad!

Bernard Why are you so prudish all of a sudden?

Jacqueline Prudish? I'm not in the least prudish.

Bernard Then don't look so stern—I mean, it's nothing to do with you if he wants to bring his girl-friend here.

Jacqueline It has everything to do with me.

Robert Of course it has. You can see it has. She's made the list, made the bed, put out the towels—expecting one person and now has to sort everything out all over again for two persons.

Bernard Pooh! Details! Not important—I think she's jealous.

Jacqueline Jealous? Me? Jealous of who?

Bernard Of her.

Robert What are you talking about?

Jacqueline Yes. What are you talking about?

Bernard Well, it's obvious. When he arrived on his own you were delighted to see him. Now that you know he's not really on his own, you're suddenly furious.

Jacqueline (*furiously*) Me? Me, furious?

Bernard Well, aren't you? If I didn't know you as well as I do I might begin to suspect that there was something going on between you.

Jacqueline Between who?

Bernard Between you two.

Jacqueline Me and Robert?

Robert Me and Jacqueline?

Bernard Yes.

Jacqueline But that's silly . . .

Robert Silly. Stupid. Absolute nonsense.

Jacqueline How on earth could there be anything between us?

Robert Quite. What about Brigit? I mean, I'm all involved with her, aren't I?

Jacqueline Yes. Apropos of Brigit—where is she?

Robert Ask Bernard.

Jacqueline Why should he know? She's your—your . . .

Bernard He did tell me, but I've forgotten.

Robert We've both forgotten.

Jacqueline How frightfully casual.

Bernard You said something about a train.

Robert Did I? Oh, yes—the train. You see, we didn't leave town at the same time. I came by car.

Bernard That's it. That's what he said—didn't you, Robert? You said she'd be coming on the train—later.

Robert I suppose so. Yes. On the train—later.

Jacqueline Which train? What time does it get in?

Robert Ah! Now I'm not quite . . .

Bernard He's not quite sure. I asked him all that before but he didn't know, did you, old chap?

Robert No. I didn't know. I didn't even know there was a train.

Bernard And because he didn't know, he told her to take a taxi when she got to the station. That's what you said, didn't you, old chap?

Jacqueline Well, if he didn't know there was a train, how did he know there was a station?

Bernard I told him.

Jacqueline But you didn't know . . .

Bernard Of course I know there's a station. And if you ask me, she's bound to be on the six-fifteen—do you think that's the one, old boy?

Robert How should I know, old chap?

Bernard Because it's the last through train.

Robert Then I expect that's the one what's-her-name will be on.

Jacqueline Brigit.

Robert Pardon?

Jacqueline Her name's Brigit.

Bernard Of course it is. So that's all perfectly clear now. Brigit will be on the six-fifteen, she'll get the taxi from the station. We'll go and do the shopping, then we'll all have the drinks and a lovely dinner together. Just the four of us. So you make yourself comfortable, old man, and we'll just whizz down to the village before the shops shut. (*He takes Robert's hat and case and puts them by the stool*)

Robert Please can I come with you?

Bernard No, you'd better stay here. She may have caught the five-ten and someone ought to be here to greet her. And as she's your girl-friend, it ought to be you. I mean, it's only polite.

Robert Yes . . .

Bernard Why don't you get the list, darling.

Jacqueline Yes. Right.

Jacqueline exits to the kitchen

Bernard There you are, old chap. Worked like a charm. What did I tell you?

Robert I think it was a mess.

Bernard I thought we carried it off very well.

Robert Jacqueline was livid.

Bernard Maybe. But none the less, you are—you're committed. And as soon as she gets here, I'm counting on you to go along with the game—the plan.

Robert But what if she turns up while you're in the village? While I'm all on my own?

Bernard (*taking his driving gloves and glasses from the hat stand*) She *will* turn up while you're on your own. I told her to catch the five-ten.

Robert Now, just a minute . . .

Jacqueline enters with her handbag and a shopping-basket

Jacqueline I'm ready, but if you want to stay with Robert, darling, I can probably manage on my own.

Bernard No, no. I wouldn't dream of it. Lots of things to carry, and it'll be faster if we both go.

Jacqueline But what's he going to do all on his own?

Bernard He can do what he likes. Watch television. Look at the garden. Ring his client and tell him to use the staircase. Whatever—the main thing is he's *not* leaving. Are you, old chap?

Robert I—I think I'll have another drink. (*He goes to the fire*)

Bernard Help yourself. See you later. (*To Jacqueline*) Come along, darling.

Bernard exits through the front door, leaving it open

Jacqueline Right away, darling. (*She turns to Robert*) I've just one thing to say to you.

Robert To me?

Jacqueline Yes, to you. I think you're the most despicable, underhand, scheming philanderer I've ever met. I despise you. I hate you. How could you?

Robert But, Jacqueline—darling . . .

Jacqueline Don't you ever "darling" me again. Save that for Brenda.

Robert Brigit. Actually, the name's Brigit.

Jacqueline I don't care! How could you? How dare you? I *hate* you!

Jacqueline exits by the front door, slamming it after her

Robert Oh dear. (*He goes to the barometer, which points at "rain", and taps it*) "Outlook Rain." I might have guessed. (*He goes to the fire and pours himself a drink. He looks at his watch and then at his suitcase, then downs his drink. He goes to the suitcase, puts on his hat, picks up the case and goes to the front door*)

The doorbell rings

Robert returns and exits down L. *A cry of annoyance escapes him, and he returns without the hat and case*

The doorbell rings again. He goes and opens the front door

Brigit stands in the doorway. She carries a large straw shopping-basket filled with unshapely parcels

Brigit Have I come to the right place?

Robert I'm afraid you have . . .

Brigit Well, that's all right then. Pleased to meet you. Good evening.

Robert Good evening.

Brigit I'm . . .
Robert Brigit.
Brigit That's right. I've come to help out.
Robert I know . . .
Brigit Just temporary—a couple of days.
Robert If you can keep it up that long.
Brigit No problem. Can I come in?
Robert Oh, certainly. Please—I didn't think you'd get here so quickly.
Brigit (*coming down into the room*) I nearly didn't get here at all—no sign of a taxi and then I'd gone and missed the bus.
Robert Really?
Brigit Yes. So I started out to walk and then some bloke came along and gave me a lift in his car.
Robert Really?
Brigit Lucky, eh? I didn't want to lug this much further, I can tell you. Can I put it down now?
Robert Oh, yes. Please do put it down.
Brigit (*sitting in the armchair with her bag on her lap*) Anyway—I hopped in the car and this bloke dropped me at the door. Much quicker in the long run than coming by bus. That's why I got here so quickly.
Robert Good.
Brigit So where is she?
Robert Where's who?
Brigit Herself. The lady of the house.
Robert She's not here. That's to say, she's gone out with himself—I mean gone out with Bernard. Shopping. She made a list.
Brigit So who are you?
Robert Me? Well, I'm Robert—Bernard's friend. Robert . . .
Brigit Pleased to meet you, I'm sure.
Robert I must get one thing clear from the beginning. And you've got to believe me. I had nothing to do with this whole preposterous idea.
Brigit What idea?
Robert Of getting you to come down here.
Brigit I was told to come on the telephone.
Robert Certainly you were. I know you were. But I have to tell you, that I find Bernard's whole approach totally despicable.
Brigit Really?
Robert I find the whole thing distasteful.
Brigit Really?
Robert Definitely. I mean, do you understand what you're letting yourself in for? It's not going to be easy, you know.
Brigit Really?
Robert Please don't keep saying "really". It's going to be jolly hard work.
Brigit (*rising*) Well, we'd better get going then, hadn't we? Where is it?
Robert Where's what?
Brigit The kitchen.
Robert What do you want to do in the kitchen?
Brigit Oh, if it's all going to be so difficult, I'd better look around and see

what's what, and what's where. Get stuck right in. I mean, what about
the vegetables?

Robert I don't know about the vegetables. I'm sure it's very nice of you to
want to help . . .

Brigit All part of the service.

Robert Very nice. But I tell you what . . .

Brigit What?

Robert I don't know where the kitchen is.

Brigit Well, let's look around and perhaps we'll find it. (*She opens the
bedroom door down* R) Not in there.

Robert Do you really think you should go poking about? It's not our
house, you know.

Brigit I know it isn't.

Robert Then maybe it would be better if we waited till they came back.

Brigit Just as you like—but I can't just hang around here chatting. If you
won't let me find the kitchen, maybe you won't mind if I get the gear on.

Robert What gear?

Brigit For getting on with the job—where can I get undressed?

Robert Undressed?

Brigit Sure. Why not. I haven't lugged all this stuff with me just for the
fun of it, you know.

Robert No?

Brigit No way.

Robert But surely you don't have to start getting undressed now?

Brigit Why not?

Robert We don't have to start pretending immediately.

Brigit Pretending what?

Robert Well—you know.

Brigit No. I'm sorry. I don't know.

Robert I'm Robert.

Brigit You said that before.

Robert I'm Bernard's friend.

Brigit I know who you are.

Robert Then you know what we have to do.

Brigit Do I?

Robert To begin with, there are lots of things you've got to know about me.

Brigit Really?

Robert Where I live, for instance. How I live.

Brigit Why have I got to know about that?

Robert It's essential. How much has Bernard told you?

Brigit About what?

Robert About me.

Brigit Nothing at all.

Robert He must be raving mad. He should have briefed you—put you in
the picture.

Brigit But it was all decided very quickly.

Robert I know that. But I didn't know anything at all until twenty
minutes ago. So we've got to work fast.

Brigit If you say so.

Robert For starters—we've got to give the impression that we know each other extremely well.

Brigit Have we?

Robert It's vital. I'm in the escalator business. I drive a Volkswagen. I'm thirty-two years old.

Brigit No kidding.

Robert Thirty-two—how old did you think I was?

Brigit I wouldn't have said you were a day past forty.

Robert I've had my appendix out.

Brigit That's nice—but what's it got to . . .

Robert The sort of thing you ought to know . . .

Brigit It's very interesting, but I don't see what it's got to do with me.

Robert A detail—small but essential. When you sleep with someone you know about things like that.

Brigit When who sleeps with who?

Robert You and me.

Brigit Look. I'm not quite sure what we're getting into here——

Robert It wasn't my idea, but now we're both here, we're going to have to sleep in the same bedroom, aren't we? But you don't have to worry about a thing—you can have the bed, I'll take the floor. Unless we can work out something else.

Brigit Like what?

Robert Well, there's another bedroom. Perhaps I can say that you've got a migraine, or I've got hay fever, something like that—anything, it doesn't really matter what—the only essential thing is that however or wherever we sleep we keep up the appearance of so-called lovers.

Brigit Why do we have to pretend to be lovers?

Robert Hasn't he told you anything?

Brigit Nothing. Nobody's told me anything at all.

Robert The man's a lunatic—how could he be so careless? You mean to say you really don't know what the plan is? What's going to happen? What you're supposed to do?

Brigit I don't know what's going to happen but I do know what I'm supposed to do—I think. The usual arrangement—board, lodging and the going rate for the job.

Robert The going rate? You mean he's actually going to pay you?

Brigit It is normal, you know, sir!

Robert Is it? I've never done it before—have you ever done it before?

Brigit I don't know if I've ever done it before—it all depends on what I'm asked to do.

Robert To pretend to be my mistress.

Brigit Just pretend to be your mistress.

Robert Pretend. Nothing more, I promise you. Pretending will be quite sufficient.

Brigit You're acting very strange, you know.

Robert I'm in a very strange position.

Brigit Why are you?

Robert Because—well, you see, it's all frightfully complicated, but Bernard doesn't know—no, I don't think I can tell you. It's too much of a muddle.

Brigit If you can't tell me, what on earth am I supposed to say?

Robert Nothing. You mustn't say anything, not a single word. Just keep quiet and watch me. If anybody asks you a question just repeat what I've said. That is, whatever I say if somebody asks me a question.

Brigit Well, I've been in some funny houses, and met some very weird people in my time. Look, I'll tell you what I'll do. If you make it worth my while, I'll go along with it.

Robert You want money?

Brigit I think all this deserves more than the going rate.

Robert Well, I didn't really think a remuneration would be involved.

Brigit Life must go on, you know.

Robert How much do you want?

Brigit It's obviously worth a good deal more than the going rate.

Robert What *is* the going rate?

Brigit Let me see. (*She starts to count on her fingers*)

A car is heard approaching

Robert Wait, wait a minute, I can hear a car. Whatever the going rate is, we'll pay you double. Bernard and I will pay you double. Right? (*He goes to the window*)

Brigit Right!

Robert Yes, yes, it's them. Their car. They're back ... Now sit down over there and look as though we've known each other very well for a very long time.

Brigit No need to panic. (*She sits with her bag as before*)

Robert Just act naturally, but not too naturally. (*He sits, then sees her bag, takes it off her lap and sits again*)

Brigit For double the going rate, I'll do anything you like.

Robert Just call me "darling".

Brigit Yes, darling.

The front door opens and Jacqueline enters carrying the shopping

Robert rushes to meet her

Robert Jacqueline, you mustn't carry all that, let me help you.

Jacqueline You keep away from me. I can manage perfectly well, thank you very much. (*She sees Brigit*) Ah. So your, your friend has arrived, has she?

Robert Yes—yes, just a minute ago. She's just arrived—haven't you, darling? You've just arrived haven't you?

Brigit (*rising*) Yes, darling. Just now, darling.

Jacqueline I think you should introduce us, Robert.

Robert Yes, of course. I'd like you to meet Brigit.

Bernard enters with another pile of parcels

Robert awkwardly puts his arm round Brigit's shoulders unaware that Bernard is trying to signal to him

Yes, Brigit—a very dear friend—that is to say, a very special sort of friend—that is to say——

Bernard becomes more and more agitated

—the fact is, we're terribly close—aren't we, darling?

Brigit Yes, I hope so, darling. (*She giggles*)

Jacqueline Yes, well I'm sure we get the message. I understand perfectly.

Brigit Well, that's all right, then.

Robert Absolutely right. Everything clear. I'd like to introduce you to Jacqueline and Bernard.

Brigit Good evening, madam.

Jacqueline Good evening.

Brigit Good evening, sir.

Surprised, Bernard looks over his shoulder, but sees nobody

Bernard Who . . .?

Brigit So what do you think of him? He's nice, isn't he?

Robert All right, darling. No need to go into all that now.

Brigit I was only going to . . .

Robert No!

Brigit I didn't want there to be any misunderstanding.

She takes his hand and swings her arm backwards and forwards. Robert shakes her off

Robert Not now, darling.

Brigit It's just that when I'm next to him, I go all to pieces.

Jacqueline How frightfully touching.

Brigit (*pushing Robert into the armchair and sitting in his lap*) I can't help it. I just can't keep my hands off him, madam.

Robert Stop it, I tell you. Stop it at once.

Brigit But when you're in your little Volkswagen, you always like it when I snuggle up real close . . .

Jacqueline How very cosy.

Robert Have you finished?

Brigit If you like . . .

Robert lifts Brigit off and rises

Robert (*to Jacqueline*) You'll have to excuse her . . .

Jacqueline Whatever for? It's rather nice to meet someone so open.

Brigit Yes, madam. I've always had a romantic nature. My Robert saw that at once when we first met.

Jacqueline Where was that?

Brigit Up one of his escalators.

Bernard I do think we ought to do something with all this shopping.

Robert Here, give them to me.

Jacqueline No, you leave them alone.

Robert But I'm only trying to help.
Brigit Course he is. I'll help too.
Jacqueline No, thank you. I'll manage on my own.
Robert If you insist.
Jacqueline I do insist.

Jacqueline exits with the shopping

Bernard wheels on Brigit

Bernard Who the hell are you?
Brigit Me?
Bernard Yes, you.
Robert What? Don't you know who she is?
Bernard Of course I don't know who she is. Didn't you see me trying to
   signal to you?
Robert Well, I could see that you were a little agitated.
Bernard Of course I was agitated. I've every right to be agitated. She's not
   her.
Brigit Of course I'm me.
Bernard You keep out of this.
Robert But if she's not her, who is she?
Bernard That's exactly what I'd like to know. (*To Brigit*) Very well then—
   who are you?
Brigit I'm his mistress.
Bernard Now look here, whoever you are—don't think you're going to
   make a monkey out of me.
Brigit But . . .
Bernard Just exactly what are you doing here?
Brigit (*to Robert*) Am I allowed to tell him?
Bernard For heaven's sake. I want to know. You've got to tell me.
Robert Yes, you've got to tell him.
Bernard I insist.
Robert So do I—we both insist.
Brigit (*to Robert*) Please, no need to shout.
Bernard All right. I won't shout. I'll ask you very nicely and very quietly.
   Where did you come from?
Brigit The agency sent me.
Robert What agency?
Brigit I thought you knew all about them.
Robert I don't know anything about anything.
Bernard Who are you? What are you?
Brigit The temporary.
Bernard The what?

*Jacqueline enters with full bottles of gin and whisky, a plate of lemons and
a box of candles*

*As she speaks Jacqueline puts the candles on the table and the bottles and
lemons by the fire*

Jacqueline The temporary hasn't arrived yet, has she? The new maid?
Brigit The maid? Well—I'm not . . .
Bernard Not—not—not yet. If she *had* arrived, she would be here.
Brigit But the new maid . . .
Bernard Hasn't come yet.
Brigit But if . . .
Bernard But if she had already come . . .
Robert I would have heard the doorbell ring.
Bernard Absolutely. He would have heard the doorbell.
Brigit But if the new maid . . .
Bernard Isn't here—it's because she's late.
Robert Quite. It happens all the time. New maids are always late.
Brigit Some may be, but . . .
Bernard But this one is obviously later than the others . . .
Brigit But . . .
Robert The whole point is that certainly, certainly the new maid ought to be here, but the fact is that she's not here.
Bernard (*to Jacqueline*) I've already asked him all this, darling, you see—while you were in the kitchen—and he told me . . .
Robert That I haven't seen the new maid.
Bernard Right.
Brigit But . . .
Bernard Besides if there was a new maid here . . .
Robert One would have heard her.
Bernard One would have seen her.
Robert One would have actually *sensed* that there was a maid in the house.
Brigit But . . .
Bernard But as nobody heard anything.
Robert And nobody saw anything.
Bernard That proves that we haven't *got* a new maid.
Robert No—we haven't got one.
Brigit We haven't got one?
Bernard And there's never been one.
Robert There's never been one.
Brigit There's never been one?
Jacqueline Please. Do you mind. Enough. Why are you making such a fuss just because the maid hasn't arrived?
Bernard You're right, darling. Much too much fuss.
Robert Sorry.
Bernard I'm sure she'll turn up eventually.
Jacqueline I'm sure she will. It's a very good agency.
Brigit One of the best.
Jacqueline How do you know?
Bernard Well, it stands to reason—when you employ staff through a good agency, you get good staff.
Robert (*to Brigit*) That's just what you were going to say, isn't it?
Brigit Yes. That's just what I was going to say.
Bernard There you are! I have this gift, you see—not all the time, but

every now and then—I can actually read people's minds. I seem to know exactly what they're going to say. Extraordinary, isn't it?

Robert Extraordinary.

Bernard Have you unpacked and all that?

Robert Not quite. Didn't quite have time. She only got here a few minutes before you returned.

Brigit Just a few minutes.

Robert But I did manage to say to her that if you had a second bedroom . . .

Brigit That's right, a second bedroom . . .

Robert And she absolutely agreed that—if it wasn't going to put you out . . .

Brigit Not put you out.

Robert She'd really much prefer . . .

Brigit To sleep in the second bedroom.

Robert Not in my bedroom. Because in the night, she gets this hay fever.

Brigit No, darling, not me. I get the migraine, *you* get the hay fever.

Robert Do I?

Brigit That's what you said.

Jacqueline No need to quarrel about it. It's perfectly simple. Where is your case?

Brigit It's there. Over there.

Jacqueline That?

Robert She believes in travelling inconspicuously.

Bernard Yes. As it's the country, there's no need to try and impress anybody.

Jacqueline No! I'll show you to your room. (*To Robert*) Perhaps you'd like to carry her bundle?

Robert Yes. Of course. (*He picks up Brigit's bag*)

Brigit It's all right, darling. I can manage. I'm used to lugging everything about.

Jacqueline Really?

Brigit I have to—all part of the job.

Jacqueline What job?

Bernard She works very hard—but then being an artist isn't all wine and roses.

Brigit An artist?

Bernard Of course you are. Isn't she, Robert?

Robert In her way, certainly . . .

Bernard Surely you recognize her? She's on the stage. Well, figuratively. What I mean is, television. That's it; you've seen her on television.

Jacqueline Doing what?

Bernard She plays maids, don't you, Brigit? Always plays maids. She's terribly good at it. What was that one last year?

Brigit I don't remember.

Robert You must do.

Brigit Must I?

Bernard You were in it.

Brigit What was I doing?

Bernard Playing a maid.
Jacqueline Did I see it?
Bernard We watched it together—that's why she calls everybody "madam" and "sir". It's become a habit, you see.
Robert And that's why she's so keen to help in the kitchen. It's catching . . .
Jacqueline What was it called?
Bernard What was what called?
Jacqueline I'm asking her!
Bernard Well, she didn't have all that much to do in it. I mean, she wasn't one of the leading characters.
Robert No, maids never are!
Brigit Oh, I don't know. What about *The Maid of Orléans*?
Robert Not in this particular play. She was just an ordinary domestic sort of maid.
Bernard Yes, she just ran around saying "Dinner is served", "Where is the potato peeler?"—all that sort of thing.
Jacqueline Well, perhaps she'd like to do part of her repertoire for us now. Recite, or something.
Brigit Dinner is served? Shall I make the beds up now?
Bernard You see! Isn't she superb?
Jacqueline Very talented—but that reminds me, I haven't made the bed up in the spare room . . .
Brigit Please, allow me, madam; must keep my hand in. Marvellous practice.
Jacqueline If you insist. This way.
Brigit After you, madam . . .

Jacqueline and Brigit exit to the bedroom up L

Bernard Idiot!
Robert I thought she did rather well.
Bernard Not her. You! You buffoon. You are the most hopeless cretin I've ever come across in my life. And when I say cretin, I'm being kind.
Robert Now don't you go turning on me. If anyone's behaving like a lunatic, it's surely you.
Bernard But don't you understand what you've done?
Robert Exactly what you told me to do. Someone rang the front doorbell. I opened the door. I saw a girl who said to me that she was called Brigit, so I thought she was your Brigit.
Bernard She doesn't look a bit like my Brigit.
Robert How was I to know?
Bernard You should have used your brains. It's written all over her. Do you think I'd choose anything like that for a mistress? You spoke to her?
Robert Yes.
Bernard Well, wasn't it obvious that she was the maid?
Robert Well, I thought a few things were a little odd . . .
Bernard How much does she know?
Robert I should think by now she knows everything.

Bernard She won't give us away?

Robert Not so long as we pay her enough.

Bernard Blackmail?

Robert Just double the going rate for the job.

Bernard How much is that?

Robert An arm and a leg—each.

Bernard Oh dear, oh dear, oh dear—a fine mess you've got me into!

Robert You! What about me! Jacqueline actually believes that I'm in love with, that I actually sleep with *that* creature.

Bernard Where's the harm in that?

Robert Well—well—it's not very nice. It makes me look such a fool.

Bernard Look like one? You're certainly behaving like one.

Robert Calling me names, old chap, isn't going to help things. So far I only look a fool, but *you*'ve got real trouble, my friend.

Brigit enters and holds the door open for Jacqueline

Brigit After you, madam.

Jacqueline (*to Robert*) There—I've made your friend as comfortable as possible.

Brigit A lovely big double bed all to myself! Because he's got this hay fever—all night long, nothing but sniffing and sneezing.

Jacqueline I know, I know, there's no need to keep on about it. Mind you, I've never known him . . . (*Quickly*) By the way—I meant to ask you, still no sign of the temporary?

Bernard No sign.

Robert Not a glimmer.

Brigit No sign of her.

Jacqueline How do you know? You weren't here with them, you were in there with me.

Brigit Ah! Yes—but this gentleman—(*pointing to Robert*)—said "not a glimmer".

Jacqueline So why do you have to echo him?

Bernard Well, she always does.

Robert In the plays—on the television, that's all maids do. Echo. They're always doing that. Always agreeing. Show her, Brigit. Do it again for her.

Jacqueline Another time. I have hundreds of things to do. I must start preparing the dinner.

Robert Brigit can go with you. Can't you, Brigit?

Brigit I'd love to. Must keep my hand in.

Jacqueline I can manage perfectly well . . .

Robert But it would give her so much pleasure.

Brigit So much pleasure . . .

Robert To help you . . .

Brigit To help you . . .

Bernard Because there's still no sign of the new maid.

Brigit Let me be the new maid.

Bernard There you are!

Robert Couldn't be simpler.

Brigit Lovely.

Jacqueline Oh, very well. Come along then. (*She goes to the kitchen door*)

Brigit I'll just put my uniform on.

Jacqueline Uniform?

Robert What she means is—just to make it look right, she'd like an apron.

Jacqueline An apron?

Bernard Yes. An apron . . .

Brigit I've got one there. (*She points to her bedroom*)

Bernard (*stepping in front of her*) There, over there. Right over there. In town!

Robert Yes, that way. Up in town . . .

Bernard She's got an apron in town.

Robert And town—well, that's that way—over there!

Brigit But . . .

Robert A very special apron—an apron that cost her two weeks' salary.

Jacqueline Two weeks?

Bernard Yes, specially made for a performance.

Robert Exactly. There you are, you see—and because it's such a special apron and it cost two weeks' salary, she didn't think it wise to bring it from town, did you, Brigit?

Brigit (*getting the point*) Ah! Yes. Two weeks' salary—I get you. Of course, that's why I didn't bring it . . .

Bernard Quite. So—if I may sum up. Because she has *not* brought her own very special and extremely expensive apron, she would like to borrow an apron.

Jacqueline I'm sure I can find something.

Brigit Nothing fancy, now . . .

Jacqueline I'll do what I can. Please—the kitchen's this way.

Brigit After you, madam.

Sighing, Jacqueline exits to the kitchen

Jacqueline (*as she goes*) Oh my God—am I going mad?

Brigit (*following*) Oh, what a beautiful kitchen. Everything! It's just like an advertisement . . .

Brigit goes through to the kitchen

Jacqueline pops back to hiss at Robert

Jacqueline My congratulations, Robert, what a quaint girl. I didn't know you were so democratic.

Jacqueline exits

Robert There, you see. Your wife thinks I'm the lover of that—that thing.

Bernard That's your look out, old man. You should have had more sense in the first place.

Robert I should have had more sense not to have listened to you in the first place.

There is a ring at the front door

Bernard What's that?
Robert It sounds like the front doorbell!
Bernard Yes, I know. I heard it.
Robert I wonder who it is?
Bernard Well, we'll know when I open the door, won't we?
Robert Yes.

Bernard opens the front door

> *Brigit 2 enters. She is wearing a mink coat and carries a little Gucci valise. She is beautifully dressed and very pretty*

Brigit 2 Well, hello!
Bernard Darling!
Brigit 2 Good evening.

Seeing Robert, she drops her valise and throws herself into his arms.

> My darling! (*Forcing him on to the sofa*) My treasure! Precious! You're here! (*She kisses him*)
Robert I say . . .
Bernard All right, all right. No need to overdo things——
Brigit 2 (*rising*) But this is Robert, isn't it?
Bernard Yes, yes, that's Robert. But you can calm down, my wife's not here . . .
Brigit 2 (*looking round*) Oh, fine. (*To Robert*) I'm sorry if I startled you.
Robert Not at all. Think nothing of it . . .

Brigit 2 goes to Bernard to embrace him

Brigit 2 My darling! My precious! Isn't this wonderfully exciting; so marvellously dangerous. . . ?
Bernard Rather more dangerous than you think. My wife isn't here, but she's around (*To Robert*) What do you think, old man?
Robert I think she's sensational.
Bernard No—do you think she'll do as the temporary?
Robert The new maid?
Bernard Why not?
Robert Doesn't quite look the part.
Bernard Then she'll have to act it.
Brigit 2 What are you two plotting?
Bernard We wouldn't have to plot if you hadn't been so late.
Brigit 2 I missed the train.
Bernard (*taking her coat off*) That was very careless—it means all the plans have to be changed.
Brigit 2 In what way?
Bernard (*putting the coat on the stool*) No time to explain all that. The essential thing is you're no longer his mistress.
Brigit 2 I'm not?
Bernard No definitely not.

Brigit 2 What am I, then?

Bernard Well—it's like this, darling, you're going to have to be . . .

Jacqueline enters briskly from the kitchen and sees Brigit 2

Jacqueline Ah, there you are and about time too.

Brigit 2 Excuse me . . .

Jacqueline I can't think why—do you know what time it is?

Brigit 2 But . . .

Bernard She's just been explaining that she unfortunately missed the . . . Well, to cut a long story short, she missed the bus.

Robert Yes, missed it completely. Missed it by hours. Didn't even see it.

Jacqueline But the agency assured me . . .

Brigit 2 The agency?

Bernard Yes, the employment agency. Domestic staff and all that . . .

Brigit 2 Domestic staff?

Jacqueline Who else would we have consulted?

Bernard Now, darling, let's not make too much of a hullabaloo. The young lady is certainly late, but there's no need for you to work yourself up into a passion about it.

Brigit 2 I'm frightfully sorry.

Bernard You see, she's frightfully sorry. Now why don't we all make the best of things and reassure her that we're frightfully glad to see her, even though she did miss the train?

Robert The bus.

Bernard What?

Robert Actually, old man, it was the bus. You said it was the bus.

Jacqueline (*seeing the mink coat*) Who does that mink belong to? (*To Brigit 2*) Is it yours?

Bernard (*leaping in*) No, no. Not hers. It belongs to Brigit, doesn't it, Robert?

Robert Yes, yes, it belongs to Brigit.

Bernard (*to Brigit 2*) Yes. Because the lady friend. That is to say the—er— the fiancée of this gentleman, by a curious coincidence is called Brigit.

Robert Yes. Astonishing, isn't it? She's also called Brigit.

Jacqueline But I didn't notice it before.

Robert Oh no—she's always been called Brigit.

Jacqueline I meant the coat! The mink! This!

Robert Oh, it must have slipped off the back of the sofa. Fallen off, isn't that so, Bernard?

Bernard Yes, yes, she must have draped it over there when she came in.

Robert That's it, that's what she did. Draped it, then it must have just— slipped.

Bernard And I saw it lying there and picked it up just before you came in. (*Robert mimes handing Bernard the mink*) Thank you.

Jacqueline But it's a beautiful coat.

Bernard Should be at that price. Isn't that what you said to me, Robert, old man?

Robert Well, I don't remember exactly . . .

Bernard Not much change out of a couple of thousand. That's what you said.

Jacqueline You surprise me, Robert. I didn't know you were so generous.

Bernard But he's always been generous. It's always been one of his nicest qualities.

Jacqueline Really? I hadn't noticed. I thought for a second that it belonged to you.

Brigit 2 (*to Bernard*) Me? Chance would be a fine thing!

Brigit 1 enters from the kitchen wearing an apron and carrying a colander of shrimps

Brigit 1 I was just wondering—what did you want me to do with the shrimps?

Jacqueline Well, now you don't have to do anything—the new maid has arrived.

Brigit 1 The new maid?

Brigit 2 I think . . .

Jacqueline (*to Brigit 1*) So you don't have to worry about the shrimps. Just give her your apron.

Brigit 1 Give her my apron?

Jacqueline You won't be needing it now. (*She takes the apron from Brigit 1 and gives it to Brigit 2*)

Jacqueline Here, put this on.

Brigit 2 I really don't think . . .

Jacqueline Please. After being so late I think the least you can do is try to co-operate. Just do as I say, and see what you can sort out in the kitchen.

Brigit 2 (*scowling at Bernard*) The kitchen?

Jacqueline Where else do you think, girl? This is hardly the time of day to begin Hoovering.

Brigit 2 I am glad to say, madam, I have never seen a Hoover.

Bernard Ha! Very witty. Did you hear that, Robert? "Never seen one." Ha!

Robert (*forced*) Ha! Ha! Did you hear that, Jacqueline?

Jacqueline (*coldly*) Yes. Very droll.

Brigit 1 (*to Jacqueline*) Listen, dear, if this one seems a little confused, I can always stay and help out in the kitchen, you know.

Jacqueline I wouldn't dream of it. There's not enough room for the three of us in there. No, I'll show her where everything is, while you put your coat in your bedroom.

Brigit My coat?

Robert Yes. Your mink coat.

Brigit 1 My mink?

Robert Your mink, which you so casually threw to the ground . . .

Bernard You should be more careful. It cost a great deal of money.

Robert So you ought to go and hang it up in your bedroom.

Brigit 1 Is it insured?

Bernard Of course it's insured.

Jacqueline How do you know?
Bernard Well, I'm in insurance. So when Robert asked me—he's my oldest friend, you know—I arranged it all for him. Didn't I, old man?
Robert So you did, old chap. (*To Brigit 1*) So you'd better look after it. Take it through there and hang it up.
Brigit 1 Yes, sir—I mean, yes, darling.

Brigit 1 exits to the bedroom up L taking the coat

Jacqueline (*to Brigit 2*) Your room, by the way, is through there, next to the kitchen.
Brigit 2 I'm not absolutely positive that . . .
Bernard Oh, you'll see! Oh, it's a sweet little room, charming, perfectly charming . . .

Brigit 1 returns

Brigit 1 That should be all right, then. I've hung it up very carefully on a hanger.
Robert Fine. Good work. Well done.
Jacqueline (*to Brigit 2*) By the way, what's your name?
Brigit 2 Brigit.
Jacqueline Ah yes—the agency did tell me.
Brigit 1 The same name as me! Now isn't that a funny thing!
Jacqueline Yes! Just to make things clear, I would like to explain that this gentleman is my husband—and this—er—gentleman is my lov—er, guest for the week-end, with this lady.
Brigit 2 Yes, I gathered all that—and I'm the new maid?
Jacqueline Well done.
Bernard But only temporary.
Jacqueline Why only temporary?
Bernard I thought that was the arrangement with the agency? All they could find was somebody temporary—I mean, for the moment she's the new maid, but I don't think that's going to last very long.
Brigit 2 I'm sure you're right, sir. Purely temporary, I assure you. I have no intention of staying . . .
Bernard Oh, I understand completely. But it really is a very pretty room. Let me show you where everything is—the light switch, the chest of drawers, the bed—and all that sort of thing. (*He picks up Brigit 2's bag*)
Brigit 2 No thank you, sir. I'll manage much better on my own. I may have difficulty with a vacuum-cleaner but I do know a *bed* when I see one!

Brigit 2 takes her bag and exits through the kitchen

Brigit 1 Well—I expect she'll take a bit of time sorting herself out so I might as well have a quick peel at the shrimps.

Brigit 1 exits to the kitchen

Jacqueline I don't think I like Brigit.
Bernard Which Brigit?

Jacqueline The pretty one—the new maid.
Bernard Oh, come on—so she was a little late, that's all.
Jacqueline Why are you making excuses for her?
Bernard Am I making excuses?
Jacqueline That's what it sounds like to me.
Bernard Well, she seems a nice enough sort of girl. Not the sort who's going to steal the silver or stuff the grouse with arsenic—and I believe in being polite. I think you were rather rude and aggressive.
Jacqueline I'm on edge. My nerves are in shreds.
Bernard Whatever for?
Jacqueline (*eyeing Robert*) Oh, nothing, nothing important, nothing at all.
Robert You've no reason to be on edge.
Jacqueline A woman always has a reason to be on edge. Anyway, I congratulate you on your taste.
Bernard His girl-friend?
Jacqueline No, her coat—very handsome.
Bernard Yes—quite superb.
Jacqueline From the Atlantic Fur Company. They're never cheap.
Bernard How did you know?
Jacqueline I read the label. I'd better go and see what the Brigits are doing —so pour me a drink will you, because I'm beginning to feel I need one.

Jacqueline exits to the kitchen

Bernard tries to pour three drinks with a shaking hand·

Robert Well, I tell you, old man, I've been in the escalator business for ten years now and I've known some very tricky moments but I've never been in a mess like this before.
Bernard The insurance business has its hairy moments—but I wouldn't like to underwrite this particular little shambles. (*He gives Robert a drink*)
Robert If I were in your shoes, old boy, I'd try to sort everything out as fast as possible. I didn't like the look in your Brigit's eyes. I mean, nice-looking girl and all that, but I wouldn't like to cross her.

Jacqueline enters with Brigit 1, who wears her apron

Jacqueline Have you fixed my drink?
Bernard Here you are, darling. Just as you like it.
Jacqueline Thank you. (*She takes the drink, and sits*)
Bernard You're very welcome, darling. And how about you, Brigit?
Brigit 1 Me? Oh, that would be very nice—I'll have a crème de menthe.
Jacqueline A what?
Brigit 1 (*to Robert*) It's a drink.
Robert Yes. But perhaps a cocktail would be more in order before dinner.
Bernard You know—a martini, or a gin and tonic.
Brigit 1 Just as you like. I'll have a port and brandy then.
Jacqueline *And* brandy?
Brigit 1 Goes down a treat (*She sits*)
Jacqueline Hardly a cocktail . . .

Bernard But very good for the voice . . .

Robert *Essential* for the voice. Opera singers knock back port and brandy all the time.

Jacqueline But they have to *sing*—they don't just trip on now and then and say "Dinner is served". You hardly need a port and brandy to say "Dinner is served".

Bernard If Brigit wants a port and brandy, she shall have a port and brandy! She's my best friend's friend.

Jacqueline Your best friend's *best* friend.

Bernard Yes. (*To Brigit 1*) So what do you want?

Brigit 1 If it's all the same to you, sir—I'd prefer a crème de menthe . . .

Bernard Oh, very well. (*He pours the drink*)

Jacqueline You know something? The more I look at you, the more I think I *did* see that piece on television.

Brigit 1 You mean you're getting used to the idea?

Bernard She rather grows on one, doesn't she? (*He hands the glass to Brigit 1*)

Brigit 1 Thanks very much.

Bernard It's a pleasure.

Brigit 2 comes from the kitchen, carrying the shrimps. She is not wearing an apron

Brigit 2 Excuse me—I just wanted to know what to do with the shrimps.

Bernard You're just in time. Perhaps you'd like to join us for an aperitif? A sherry or something?

Brigit 2 But sir—I don't think it would be quite correct.

Bernard Perfectly correct, I assure you.

Jacqueline Absolutely. My husband has asked you, and it's only correct that you do as he asks.

Bernard Quite. So what can I offer you?

Brigit 2 If you insist—I'll have a vodka martini, straight up with just a kiss of vermouth and . . .

Bernard Don't tell me! Not an olive—a twist of lemon.

Brigit 2 Yes . . .

Jacqueline How did you know?

Bernard It's this gift. (*He pours the drink*)

Jacqueline Tell me something. I didn't mention it earlier but I've been wondering where you got that dress, it looks very—very chic.

Brigit 2 Oh, it's nothing much.

Bernard (*mixing and passing the martini*) Nothing much, nothing at all—couldn't have cost more than . . .

Brigit 2 I don't know how much it cost, sir. (*She gives Bernard the shrimps*) It was a present.

Bernard puts the shrimps on the table

Robert Well, if it was a present, it's not really polite to inquire how much it costs.

Brigit 2 sits

Brigit 1 If it's a present, all I can say is, well done, girl . . . Let the gentlemen pay, that's what I always say . . . (*She lifts her glass to Jacqueline*) Don't you think so, madam?

Jacqueline Certainly. I was never mercenary before, but I intend to be extremely grasping in the future.

Brigit 1 Good for you, dear. I'll drink to that. Better days.

They all clink glasses and drink

Ooooh! That does taste nice. Really hit the spot it has.

Jacqueline I'm so glad.

Brigit 1 Nothing like a crème de menthe to perk you up.

Jacqueline (*rising*) Well—I'm not going to get dinner cooked and served just sitting round here and chatting—however brilliant the conversation.

Robert Could I be of any assistance?

Jacqueline I don't think so. We are already . . .

Brigit 1 Three women looking after two men. "Turkish delight", as my mother used to say. (*She giggles*)

Robert I think you should have a little more ice with your crème de menthe. (*To Jacqueline*) There must be something two strong fellows like us could do to help.

Jacqueline Well, you could open up that folding table and put it over there.

Brigit 1 (*rising*) Oh, no, I'll do it. I don't like to see gentlemen shifting things when I'm about. (*She puts the records from the table with the others*)

Jacqueline I didn't know you people took your roles quite so seriously. I didn't think you'd be wanting to rehearse all the time.

Brigit 1 moves the table to the middle of the room

Robert No. Exhausting, isn't it? (*To Bernard*) For God's sake give her some more ice!

Jacqueline You don't have to help.

Brigit 1 Oh, I do it all the time, dear. (*She clears the table except for the shrimps, lifts up the flap, takes a duster from the table drawer, and dusts the top*)

Robert (*aside to Bernard*) Better she should help than drown herself in the crème de menthe. (*To Brigit 1*) If you insist, dear—you trot along and see what you can do. (*He pushes her towards the kitchen*)

Brigit 1 Righty ho! One volunteer's worth ten pressed men—that's what my mother always used to say.

Robert She must have been an amazing woman—a positive mine of repartee!

Brigit 1 She wouldn't have had much time for *you*, darling. She'd have had a shotgun at your back. Didn't approve of hanky-panky . . .

Brigit 1 exits to the kitchen with the shrimps

Jacqueline (*to Brigit 2*) She seems determined to take your place. I'm sorry . . .

Brigit 2 It's all the same to me, madam.

Jacqueline Well, if it wouldn't upset Mr Robert's friend, perhaps you could start laying the table?

Brigit 2 Very well, madam.

Jacqueline I'm going to see what she's up to with those shrimps.

Jacqueline exits to the kitchen

Brigit 2 (*to Bernard*) You must be very pleased with yourself.

Bernard But, my darling, precious, listen to me . . .

Brigit 2 Let's get one thing clear, I'm telling you here and now that I'm not going to stand this much longer . . .

Bernard (*to Robert*) Now do you understand what you've done?

Robert Me? Oh, suddenly it's all my fault, is it?

Brigit 2 Totally. If you hadn't mistaken her for me . . .

Robert Well, he ought to have told me that she was coming before you.

Brigit 2 But she isn't a bit like me.

Robert Absolutely. Not a bit like you. But I didn't know that, did I? Because I'd never met you.

Brigit 2 It's so humiliating. (*She takes six serving mats from the table and starts to lay them*)

Robert It's humiliating for all of us.

Bernard (*moving to the table*) But it's much more humiliating for her, old man. You're still Robert, but she's got to play a maid.

Brigit 2 I should never have come here, not even if it is my birthday . . .

Bernard (*leaning towards her over the table*) We'll work something out, darling.

Brigit 2 But how?

Bernard I don't know how, not yet. But I'll think of something. You'll just have to trust me.

Brigit 2 I don't know about trust you, but I do love you, you know that. (*She is about to kiss him*)

Jacqueline enters from the kitchen

Robert swiftly steps up behind Bernard and swings his head round

Jacqueline Bernard, where's the . . . ? What on earth are you doing?

Bernard Nothing, nothing at all, darling. There was something stinging. Wasn't there, Robert?

Robert Yes, stinging. Very nasty. Got him round just in time. Whatever it was that was stinging must have gone somewhere else.

Jacqueline How do you know that?

Bernard Elementary. It's not bothering him any more.

Robert And if it's not bothering him any more, then whatever it was must have gone somewhere else. Must have been in insect. A little tiny insect. So tiny that Brigit couldn't see it. But we *are* in the country after all, so you must expect insects. Perhaps you ought to spray?

Jacqueline Oh, shut up. Ah, you've laid the mats. What else is there . . . Ah yes—the napkins. (*To Brigit 2*) You'll find them in the bottom left-hand drawer.

Brigit 2 Very well, madam.

Jacqueline And if they're not in the bottom left-hand drawer, then they're most probably in the top right-hand drawer. Anyway, I'm sure you know a napkin when you see one. Perhaps you'd be good enough to look.

Brigit 2 Yes, madam.

Brigit 2 exits into the kitchen

Jacqueline And I think it's time you two changed for dinner. Have you brought your dinner jacket?

Robert Well, yes. Bernard asked me to. But I'm not quite sure about . . .

Jacqueline About who?

Bernard He's not sure if his Brigit has brought anything. An evening dress, that is.

Brigit 1 enters from the kitchen

Brigit 1 Sorry to trouble you . . .

Jacqueline What is it?

Brigit 1 What do you want me to do with the mussels? Poach them, or stuff them with garlic and parsley?

Jacqueline Parsley's fine. Garlic might be a little strong—overpower the shrimps.

Brigit 1 That's just what I was thinking—so I'll just brew them up in a bit of white wine. Very tasty. (*She turns back towards the kitchen*)

Bernard Just a minute, Brigit. Did you think to bring another dress with you?

Brigit 1 My frock? Oh, yes, it's in with all the rest of my gear.

Bernard That's fine—isn't it, Robert?

Robert Fine, first class. Splendid.

Brigit 1 Do you want me to start putting it on now?

Bernard No rush—later.

Robert Later. Later.

Brigit 1 Right. Right you are. Later. So I'll get back to my mussels . . .

Jacqueline How very kind. And you'll find the plates in the sideboard—left-hand side at the top.

Brigit 1 You just leave it all to me, madam. I know where they are.

Brigit 1 exits to the kitchen

Robert Don't forget the parsley!

Jacqueline So that's all settled. (*To Bernard*) Why don't you run along and change now?

Bernard In a minute, darling. I can't leave dear old Robert all on his own . . .

Robert But I'll go and change now too, if you like.

Bernard Fine. Let's both go and change.

Jacqueline No. We'll each change in turn. Like that, nobody will be left on their own.

Bernard Just as you like, angel. I won't be a jiffy.

Bernard exits to the bedroom down R

Jacqueline I'm amazed you're not *petrified* with shame by now.
Robert Jacqueline, I beg you—please keep calm.
Jacqueline Keep calm! In the circumstances, I think I'm keeping remarkably calm.
Robert Then please don't shout.
Jacqueline I'm not shouting—not yet!
Robert He'll hear us!

Brigit 1 enters suddenly from the kitchen, with four side plates, four dessert plates and four dinner plates

Brigit 1 Aha!
Jacqueline Aha—what?
Brigit 1 Just—aha! I've brought the plates, that's all. Aha. . . .
Jacqueline Just put them on the table.
Brigit 1 Should I lay the places? (*She starts to lay them out*)
Jacqueline No, just leave them.
Brigit 1 But it's just as easy to set them out.
Jacqueline No. I'll set them out.
Brigit 1 Just leave them here? (*She puts the rest of the plates down*)
Jacqueline Yes.
Brigit 1 Just in a pile?
Jacqueline Yes.
Brigit 1 (*picking the plates up*) It wouldn't take a moment to . . .
Jacqueline Please. Just put them down in a pile. Just as they are.
Brigit 1 Just as you like. (*She leaves the plates on the table and goes to Robert*) And how about you, darling?
Robert What about me?
Brigit 1 Are you enjoying yourself, darling?
Robert Yes. Having a simply wonderful time.
Brigit 1 That's nice—so give us a kiss then, darling.
Robert Not now.
Brigit 1 (*to Jacqueline*) You wouldn't mind, would you, madam? Not going to upset you or anything like that?
Jacqueline Why on earth should it upset me? (*She looks towards the kitchen and sniffs*) What was happening in the kitchen when you left?
Brigit 1 Oh Lord—must be the mushrooms. That's the trouble with electric stoves—they don't understand the vegetables like the gas does. Hold on! I'll be right there.

Brigit 1 exits to the kitchen

Jacqueline I'm fed up to the teeth with that one. You've really picked yourself a dazzler there! (*She begins to lay out the plates—testily*)
Robert Jacqueline, darling, I implore you . . .
Jacqueline You can save your breath. I don't wish to discuss anything with you—except to ask where on earth did you find her?
Robert If only I could explain.
Jacqueline There is nothing to explain. I don't wish to hear it.
Robert If only you'd listen to me . . .

Jacqueline Never again . . . (*She sets a chair at the table*)

Robert I should never have agreed to come here. You and I, together, actually under Bernard's nose—hardly politic, rather distasteful.

Jacqueline You weren't so fussy when we saw each other in town.

Robert Right. But in town it didn't seem so distasteful. But here, in the country, in your house—that is, in his house. Well, it all seems a little sordid.

Jacqueline How dare you use that word. The only thing sordid in this house at this moment is that you've seen fit to import your mistress!

Robert But she's not my mistress!

Jacqueline I see. I suppose now you're going to start telling me that she's your long lost cousin, or your niece—well, you're wasting your time.

Jacqueline exits to the bedroom up L

Robert No. You've hit the problem right on the spot. That's exactly it. She's my niece. That is, well, exactly what you said—I'm her uncle.

Jacqueline returns with a chair

Jacqueline Oh, for goodness sake! Stop it, will you! (*She sets the chair at the table*)

Robert I can't stop now, don't you see, that's exactly why she didn't want to sleep in the same room with me.

Jacqueline She didn't want to sleep in the same room as you because you spend all night wheezing and sneezing—keeps your girl-friend from getting a wink of sleep.

Robert Not my girl-friend, my niece.

Jacqueline If she's your niece, how does your niece know that you sneeze all night?

Robert Because I'm her uncle.

Jacqueline You never sneeze in bed with me. (*She picks up another chair*)

Robert Ah, but that's in town, I only get hay fever in the country, so I only sneeze in the country . . . (*He sneezes*)

Jacqueline God bless you. (*She sets the chair at the table*)

Robert Thank you. You see, your Bernard thought it a little odd that I always seem to be on my own. So when he invited me down here, I thought it wise to bring my niece.

Jacqueline Well, why haven't you told him she's your niece?

Robert That's the trick of it. That's where the politics come in. If he thinks she's my mistress, then he's not going to start getting ideas about the relationship between you and me—is he?

Jacqueline No—I didn't see it like that . . . No, darling, now you've explained things I can only ask you to forgive me. I didn't understand. I should have trusted you.

They go to kiss each other

Robert Of course you should——

Jacqueline My brave, brave boy! My big, bold lion! (*She kisses him*)

Brigit 1 enters suddenly from the kitchen, with a tray of cutlery

Brigit 1 Aha!

Jacqueline What is it now?

Brigit 1 (*putting the tray on the table*) I've sorted out most of the cutlery, but I can't find any fish knives or forks. (*She advances on Robert*) And my darling little Robby is very finicky about all that sort of thing. Likes everything to be proper, don't you, darling?

Jacqueline You don't have to force yourself any more. I know everything.

Brigit 1 Everything? Everything about what?

Jacqueline He's told me all about you.

Brigit 1 (*astonished*) Aha! So you know that I'm . . .

Robert (*jumping in*) My little Brigit.

Brigit 1 Your little Brigit?

Jacqueline I know he's your Uncle Bob.

Brigit 1 My uncle?

Jacqueline Yes.

Robert Your uncle.

Brigit 1 Aha! If that's how it is—Uncle Bob it is. Hello, Uncle Bob. I'm glad it's all been made clear because I need a bit of help, Uncle Bob.

Robert Anything you like.

Brigit 1 Then I think we'll have to review the going rate, Uncle Bob.

Jacqueline What is she saying?

Robert Oh, it's just something from way back. A family joke.

Brigit 1 Yes. He always used to make us laugh so much when we were little. He was always so kind, and so generous. Never forgot a birthday.

Robert I'll never forget this one.

Jacqueline Oh, is it somebody's birthday?

Brigit 1 Not mine, dear.

Robert Not mine.

Jacqueline And it's certainly not Bernard's. (*She goes to the fireplace and puts two candles in the candlesticks*)

Brigit 1 With all that food we've got going out there, it seems to me it's more like a coronation.

Jacqueline Yes, we mustn't forget the dinner. I'll finish laying the table with Brigit while you nip off and change.

Robert At once. If you'll be kind enough to keep an eye on my little niece.

Brigit 1 (*moving back to square one*) Your niece?

Robert If I'm your Uncle Bob, what does that make you?

Brigit 1 Your little niece!

Robert Right. Won't be long!

Brigit 1 You take your time, Uncle. I won't let you down—must keep up the family reputation, and all that.

Robert moves to the bedroom door down L *and, as Jacqueline has her back to him, he makes tic-tac signs to Brigit 1—flashing his fingers to indicate the agreed price. Brigit 1—bookmaker-fashion—signals back when the price is high enough by drawing her finger across her throat. Robert visibly blanches and signals his agreement*

Robert exits down L

Jacqueline (*starting to lay cutlery*) I'm very grateful for all you're doing.

Brigit 1 (*helping, and polishing the cutlery*) Oh, it's nothing at all, I enjoy this—the knives and forks and spoons.

Jacqueline Nothing to do with the spoons. I wanted to thank you for helping us out—for having agreed to act as a screen.

Brigit 1 A screen?

Jacqueline Yes. Because nobody knows that you're his niece—and when I say "nobody", I'm sure you know exactly who I mean.

Brigit 1 Yes . . .

Jacqueline And nobody doubts for a minute that you're not Robert's mistress—that's what I mean by your being a screen. I can't thank you enough.

Brigit 1 Well, I've been called a lot of things in my time.

Brigit 2 enters from the kitchen with four napkins in rings

Brigit 2 I've found the napkins, madam. Can you imagine where I found them . . .?

Jacqueline (*laying the napkins in place*) No idea. The main thing is you *did* find them. Now what else do we need? Ah! the glasses. (*To Brigit 1*) Do you know where they are?

Brigit 1 No. But I'll find them wherever they are.

Jacqueline Thank you. I'm going to leave everything to you. (*To Brigit 2*) You can finish arranging all that with her.

Brigit 2 Very good, madam.

Jacqueline I'm going to change.

Jacqueline exits down R

Brigit 2 Now look—I simply can't go on taking your place.

Brigit 1 (*picking up the napkins and removing the rings*) But I've gone and taken yours.

Brigit 2 In what way?

Brigit 1 (*sitting and folding the napkins in fancy shapes*) Well, you've been introduced as the new maid, and as there can't be two new maids . . .

Brigit 2 But you were here first, and you're the real one.

Brigit 1 Yes. I know that. But it's only those who are in the know who actually know . . .

Brigit 2 But it's nothing to do with you—not really. So why are you letting yourself go along with it all? Why do you let yourself be pushed about?

Brigit 1 I'm not being pushed about by nobody. No-one pushes me about unless they're prepared to pay for it. I'm simply earning my living. What the rest of you get up to is none of my business, is it? After all, I'm not here to reform the world. I'm only temporary. Just passing through. A spectator, if you know what I mean. But whatever you're up to my dear, I hope you're not going to start blowing the cover now, or knocking over the screens—because I'm one of the screens and I'm getting very well paid for it.

Bernard enters, wearing a dress shirt and the trousers of his dinner jacket

Bernard Nothing wrong, is there?

Brigit 1 Everything's fine.

Brigit 2 Everything's not fine. For a start . . .

Brigit 1 Yes, for a start, she wants me to own up to being the temporary.

Bernard But she can't! And she won't!

Brigit 1 It would be a bit difficult now—it's all rolling along so smoothly. (*She replaces the napkins*)

Brigit 2 Speak for yourself. I don't find it smooth at all.

Bernard But my darling, everything will sort itself out in a flash. You'll see. Just answer one question Simply yes or no.

Brigit 1 Just like the television.

Bernard Not a bit like the television.

Brigit 1 Are there any prizes?

Bernard Double the going rate—arms and legs—you name it.

Brigit 1 Then I'm ready . . .

Bernard Quickly then. Here's the question. Would you mind sleeping tonight in the little bedroom beside the kitchen?

Brigit 1 For another arm and a leg, I'd sleep in the fridge . . . An arm and a leg at the going rate, that is.

Bernard You've got it. It's a deal. (*To Brigit 2*) There you go. You two can change rooms later. (*To Brigit 1*) But not a word to my wife.

Brigit 1 Why not?

Bernard Because it's just not normal that the maid—this Brigit here— sleeps in the best bedroom, while you—my best friend's best friend— look, let's not get into all that again. If it's too complicated for you, don't worry about it—just do it. (*Looking at the table*) Have you finished with all this?

Brigit 1 No. We need glasses.

Bernard Glasses . . .

Brigit 1 So does she go and look for them, or do I go?

Bernard You go.

Brigit 1 So I'm back to being the new maid?

Bernard No. You're a guest who just happens to be helping.

Brigit 2 Because *I'm* the new maid.

Brigit 1 (*picking up the cutlery tray*) Got it, dear. That's exactly what I told you a moment ago, but you wouldn't believe me. Right, so now all that's sorted out—I'm going to hunt up the glasses. Won't be a tick . . .

Brigit 1 exits to the kitchen

Bernard There, you see, darling, all worked out—expensively, but rather neatly. You're going to have the most beautiful bedroom and an enormous comfortable bed.

Brigit 2 And you'll arrange everything else? That I can be with you all evening and all through the night?

Bernard I swear it.

Brigit 2 And do you love me?

Bernard You know I do. How could you ask such a question?

Brigit 2 I thought you'd gone off me a bit.

Bernard Never, never, never. I adore you—mad about you! (*He takes her in his arms and is about to kiss her*)

Jacqueline enters, in evening dress

Jacqueline Bernard!
Bernard (*jumping*) Aie, aie, aie . . .
Jacqueline What are you doing?
Bernard What am I doing? She just trod on my foot.
Jacqueline Well, you shouldn't get in her way. There's lots of work to do, you know. And shouldn't you—(*to Brigit 2*)—be helping Brigit polish the glasses rather than trampling all over my husband?
Brigit 2 At once, madam. So sorry, sir.

Brigit 2 exits to the kitchen

Jacqueline Is it broken?
Bernard Is what broken?
Jacqueline Your foot.
Bernard No, no—frightfully painful, but only bruised. I expect I shall limp a bit.
Jacqueline She's only a slip of a thing.
Bernard Yes, but very bony. Pretty, though—and young.
Jacqueline Yes . . . I may just have to strangle her!

Robert enters, wearing his dinner jacket

Robert Here I am—all ready.
Jacqueline And very nice you look.
Bernard Superb, old man, quite superb.
Robert Thank you. You're also looking rather . . .
Jacqueline It's because he's just been injured.
Robert I say . . .
Jacqueline We may have to get him a crutch.
Robert Really?
Jacqueline The new maid just trod on his foot. I must go and see what's happening in the kitchen.

Jacqueline exits to the kitchen

Robert Is it painful, old man?
Bernard It's just a cover. Now, you've got to help me . . .
Robert Well, I don't know about a crutch, but if you had an axe or a knife I could go and chop you a walking stick.
Bernard Forget it. Nothing wrong with my foot at all. Just forget the foot. What you've got to do, is to persuade Jacqueline to ask Brigit to have dinner with us.
Robert Why?
Bernard Because I can't let her sit all on her own in the kitchen while the real maid sits down at table with us.
Robert But why do I have to ask Jacqueline? Why is it always me? What on earth am I going to say?

Bernard I don't know . . .

Robert There are some things you really ought to do for yourself.

Bernard But I can't—this one I have to leave to you. If I ask Jacqueline to ask the maid to have dinner with us, it would look suspicious, but if you ask her to ask her it'll seem in character. Normal. She knows you're a bit eccentric, you see.

Robert I was never eccentric until you made me eccentric. I've been normal for thirty-two years. It's only since this afternoon that I've turned eccentric, and it's all your fault.

Jacqueline enters, with a cheque book

Jacqueline Bernard! Where on earth have you hidden the champagne?

Bernard I wanted to get it chilled.

Jacqueline Then why not put it in the fridge?

Bernard There wasn't room. But never mind, I know where it is. Just leave it to me, angel.

Bernard exits to the kitchen

Jacqueline glides towards Robert

Jacqueline You've said nothing about my dress.

Robert Because I'm overwhelmed. Speechless, darling. You look—you look ravishing.

She slaps him across the face

Jacqueline Liar!

Robert You struck me. What did you do that for?

Jacqueline Because you've lied to me.

Robert About what?

Jacqueline About everything. Look what I've found. (*She produces a cheque book*) You see this?

Robert reaches out for the cheque book. She slaps him across the back of the hand with the cheque book

No. Don't touch. Evidence.

Robert If I'm not allowed to look . . .

Jacqueline It's a cheque book. Any fool can see it's a cheque book. The question is, *whose* cheque book?

Robert (*ducking*) Yours?

Jacqueline Not mine—Bernard's! And the stub of cheque number three-two-one stroke oh-oh-five, dated the twenty-fifth—that's three days ago —is made out to the Atlantic Fur Company!

Robert How—how much?

She shows him the cheque book

Phew! That's an awful lot of money.

Jacqueline Mink coats cost an awful lot of money.

Robert Mink? You don't mean to imply . . .

Jacqueline I most certainly do. "Not much change out of two thousand."
The cheque is for the mink coat that belongs to your niece.

Robert Not that mink?

Jacqueline Is there another mink in the house? Mine is up in town.
Perhaps the new maid has one?

Robert Then it's a coincidence—an extraordinary coincidence!

Jacqueline Rubbish. (*She moves to hit him again with the cheque book*)

*Bernard enters carrying two bottles of champagne in buckets, one bottle
opened*

Bernard Here we are then! (*He puts one bucket by the sofa*) Found the fizz!
No problem! And they're cold. Absolutely glacial.

Jacqueline (*sitting and hiding the cheque book under the sofa cushion*) Good.

Robert How did you manage it, old man. Where were they? In the cellar?
And how's your foot? Ice is awfully effective, you know——

Bernard (*putting the bucket with the open bottle on the table*) The foot's
cured; just fine. But is anything the matter with you? You look rather
furtive.

Robert Who does? She does?

Bernard No. You does—do—both of you—do—does . . . Perhaps you
were talking about the new maid?

Jacqueline (*rising*) Why should we be talking about her?

Bernard Robert was going to—I thought he wanted to . . .

Robert Do keep it quiet. She may hear us.

Jacqueline What does it matter if she does hear us?

Bernard He wanted it to be a surprise.

Robert Yes. Wouldn't be the same if it wasn't a surprise.

Jacqueline What surprise? I don't like surprises. I've had enough surprises for one day.

Bernard Not you, darling. He was thinking of the new maid.

Jacqueline What about her?

Robert Well, it's going to be a bit sad for her——

Bernard Having to eat by herself——

Robert In a little corner by the sink——

Bernard In the kitchen——

Robert All alone——

Bernard A young girl like her——

Robert Who so dislikes her vocation——

Jacqueline Wait a moment—whose idea is this?

Robert } His. { (*Speaking together*)
Bernard

Jacqueline I see! So I can't really object—especially if it would give you
pleasure.

*Brigit 2 enters from the kitchen with a little tray of salt cellars and pepper
mills*

Brigit 2 I thought you'd be needing these, madam.

Jacqueline Thank you, Brigit, just put them down on the table.

Brigit 2 does so

Tell me—we were wondering if you'd like to join us for dinner—would that amuse you?

Bernard All we have to do is find another chair. (*He goes to the stool*) It couldn't be simpler!

Robert No. It couldn't be simpler.

Jacqueline Well, Brigit?

Brigit 2 Well, yes. Thank you very much. It'll mean a lot to me, you see, because today—well, it's my birthday.

Robert } Your birthday! { (*Speaking together*)
Bernard }

Jacqueline How very strange. Someone was talking about a birthday a few minutes ago.

Brigit 2 Perhaps you'd like me to change?

Bernard (*placing the stool at the table*) That would be perfect—you've brought a dress?

Jacqueline Something suitable for a dinner party?

Brigit 2 I think so, madam.

Jacqueline Then you'd better go and put it on.

Brigit 2 At once—and thank you so much for inviting me. I'm quite overcome and very grateful.

Brigit 2 exits to the kitchen

Jacqueline You know—I've never seen a temporary like that before.

Robert } Neither have I. { (*Speaking together*)
Bernard }

Brigit 1 enters with a tray of glasses

Jacqueline (*aggressively*) You again!

Brigit 1 Is there anything wrong?

Bernard No, nothing's wrong—everything's in excellent order.

Brigit 1 sets the glasses on the table

Brigit 1 I polished them up. They were in a terrible state—covered in dust and Lord knows what.

Jacqueline I'm sorry . . .

Brigit 1 And murder to wash. The stems keep snapping off. But then, what do you expect from cheap glasses?

Bernard Cheap? What do you mean, cheap? They were a wedding present.

Jacqueline Never mind, no time to go into all that now. (*To Brigit 1*) You're not yet dressed.

Brigit Aren't I?

Jacqueline For dinner. Surely you've brought something to wear for dinner?

Brigit 1 Oh me, I've always got something for everything, I have.

Robert Then go and put it on.

Jacqueline Yes. Go and change.

Brigit 1 Look. I'm not here to argue with—I don't want to contradict anybody, but . . .

Bernard There's nothing to argue about, just go and change.

Robert Do as the man says.

Brigit 1 All right, all right, I'm going. No need to snap my head off, you know. I'm a guest, I am—even if I *am* cooking the dinner and up to my armpits in parsley!

Brigit 1 exits to the bedroom up L, muttering

Bernard I'd better put on my jacket. I won't be long.

Bernard exits to the bedroom down R

Jacqueline (*attacking Robert*) Good! So you're not only a liar, but now you're a hypocrite!

Robert Am I?

Jacqueline It's sickening—the fact that Bernard bought that mink coat for your odious niece makes it crystal clear . . .

Robert Makes what clear?

Jacqueline That your niece is Bernard's girl-friend. His mistress!

Robert Oh, come on, you don't know what you're saying.

Jacqueline I know what I'm saying. I happen to be the only person telling the truth this evening!

Robert So she has a mink coat? Why should you decide that it was given to my niece by your Bernard? Why should he?

Jacqueline Because he's her lover. And when he asked you to bring her down here and pass her off as *your* mistress, it was just a cover—a screen—so that I wouldn't get suspicious, so that I wouldn't put two and two together and find out that she was really *his* mistress.

Robert Jacqueline! My darling! You've always had a wild imagination, but what you're saying is incredible. Fantastic and impossible.

Jacqueline I know I'm right.

Robert But, darling . . .

Jacqueline And I'm going to prove it. You haven't seen anything yet. Just you wait till I'm good and ready!

Bernard enters, wearing his dinner jacket

Bernard Here we are! All ready, and as hungry as a hunter.

Jacqueline (*coolly*) Then let's sit down.

Bernard Don't you think we should wait for the others?

Brigit 1 enters. She is wearing a little maid's dress in dark silk with a little frilly apron

Brigit 1 Well, here I am!

Jacqueline (*stupefied*) But what on earth have you got on?

Bernard and Robert are equally amazed, but Robert quickly pulls himself together. He starts to laugh

Robert Ha! ha! Now I really like that! Marvellous, Brigit. You are a hoot . . .

Bernard That's it! A hoot! Well I never, what will you think of next? (*To Jacqueline*) Isn't she a scream?

Jacqueline Not exactly. She doesn't make *me* laugh.

Robert But it's her costume, her maid's outfit.

Jacqueline I thought you said that she said that her apron was up in town —that way.

Bernard But not her evening apron.

Jacqueline Is it absolutely vital for her to put on her costume whenever she goes out to dinner?

Brigit 1 Absolutely.

Jacqueline How exhausting!

Robert It always makes people laugh.

Bernard I think it's marvellous.

Brigit 1 (*to Bernard, coyly*) I'm glad only *you* seem to be so pleased.

Jacqueline Seem? Surely you can see that he's pleased—after all . . .

Robert After all, she's a bundle of tricks is Brigit. Like the magician— now you see it, now you don't. All done by mirrors! All up the sleeve!

Brigit 1 What are you going on about?

Robert nudges Bernard and points to Brigit. Both men advance on her

Robert Abracadabra.

Brigit 1 What are you doing? . . . Keep away from me . . . I don't like the look . . . Here! Do you mind! . . . Keep off!

Robert and Bernard grab hold of Brigit 1, turn her round a couple of times like a top, and then start to work on her dress. Robert turns the apron round her waist, and Bernard starts to transform it into a large butterfly bow. Robert attacks the neckline of the dress, pulling and ripping until it achieves a décolleté effect. Then each one rips off a sleeve to get a bare arm effect, then both kneel and attack the skirt—ripping away at the hem until it is transformed into a long evening dress. Bernard gets a rose from a vase and pops it in her cleavage. Finally, the metamorphosis achieved, they spin Brigit round a couple of times, and then present her to Jacqueline

At this moment Brigit 2 enters from the kitchen dressed in a magnificent evening gown. She carries a large silver plate which is heaped with sea food and topped by three large lobsters—the same colour as her dress

Brigit 2 Ladies and gentlemen—dinner is served. (*She puts the dish on the table*)

Bernard and Robert light the candles on the table, moving below it. Brigit 2 moves below the table and sits with her back to the audience, revealing that her dress is extremely low cut, and that it is amazingly tight over the bottom. Both Bernard and Robert do a double take at the vision

Bernard Let's get at it, then! (*He pours four glasses of champagne*)

Robert Pardon . . . ? The dinner. Looks good enough to eat . . .

Bernard I'm talking about the lobsters . . .

Jacqueline (*to Robert*) What were *you* talking about?

Robert Oh! Certainly. The lobsters. Magnificent!

Bernard (*raising his glass*) Happy Birthday, Brigit!

All Happy Birthday . . .

There is an ominous rumble of thunder, followed by a flash of lightning outside the window. They all look at one another

Brigit 1 Well, you make the most of it, girl. If I read the signs right, we're in for a dirty night!

CURTAIN

ACT II

The same. That night, after dinner

As the CURTAIN *rises, there is a distant rumble of thunder. The dinner table has been cleared away. It is now dark outside and the lamps in the living room are alight. The front door is open*

Robert and Bernard are discovered together. Both have discarded their jackets and it is plainly very warm. Robert is fanning himself with a record sleeve

Robert (*sitting by the fireplace with a pile of records*) Which do you prefer? Funky rock or blues?

Bernard (*standing at the front door*) I never know the difference. Anyway, you can leave the music for the moment.

Robert But Jacqueline asked me to choose—to put something on the record player.

Bernard (*moving to the kitchen door*) It's far too hot for dancing. (*He opens the door, looks in, then closes it again*)

Robert I agree. There's going to be a storm.

Bernard (*shutting the front door*) You said that before, but it hasn't happened.

Robert Before I was speaking metaphorically—but now you can feel it coming. It's frightfully muggy and close.

Bernard All that food and drink—I don't think I could dance to save my life.

Robert But you suggested it in the first place, old man!

Bernard Yes, old chap, but only as a pretext to get the dinner table and things cleared away—so that you and I could have a couple of minutes together to work out a solution.

Robert Solution? How can there be a solution to the mess you're in?

Bernard The mess we're both in—and I'm very worried about Brigit.

Robert Which Brigit?

Bernard My Brigit. She's been desperate ever since she arrived, and I just can't abandon her now.

Robert She did have rather a lot to drink at dinner.

Bernard It's her birthday.

Robert I know. But isn't it dangerous? Alcohol loosens the tongue and all that . . . And there's something I have to tell you——

Bernard Oh, nothing else is important. I must be with her tonight—just the two of us alone together. So as soon as they come back yawn, say you're tired, say you have to go to bed.

Brigit 1 enters from the kitchen with a large glass of crème de menthe and ice. She is wearing her apron

Brigit 1 Would either of you gentlemen like coffee?

Bernard I'd love some. How about you, old man?

Robert Fine—but I'm supposed to be sleepy. Won't keep me awake, will it?

Bernard Might keep you on your toes—metaphorically. (*To Brigit 1*) He'll have coffee too.

Brigit 1 Right. (*She moves towards the kitchen*)

Bernard Brigit!

Brigit 1 Yes?

Bernard Have you finished the washing up?

Brigit 1 Getting on.

Bernard How's it going?

Brigit 1 Not too bad—only three plates and half a dozen glasses broken so far.

Bernard Mind you don't give anything away.

Brigit 1 If I give anything away, it'll only be because I don't know as much about everything as what you two do. I'm only passing through. I get a bit lost now and then.

Bernard You're doing very well. Just keep it like that.

Brigit 1 Don't you worry, sir. I'll hang in there. And what about the coffee? You still want it?

Robert Yes, please.

Brigit 1 Right you are, Uncle. Two coffees it is. Won't be a tick.

Brigit 1 exits to the kitchen

Bernard What did she say?

Robert That she won't be a tick.

Bernard No. I'm asking why she called you "uncle"?

Robert Uncle? Did she?

Bernard I heard her. She called you "uncle".

Robert I expect that's because she's a temporary. I mean, if they're hopping from one house to another, here one day another family the next, it must be very difficult for them. I expect they get confused. (*He puts the records away, retaining one*)

Bernard I just hope she remembers why we're paying her. She's being paid Lord knows how many times the going rate, plus half-a-dozen arms and legs, in order to pass herself off as your mistress.

Robert I'm sure she understands that. By the way, how much is an arm and a leg these days?

Bernard How should I know?

Robert You're in insurance.

Bernard We'll work it out later. That's only money—but I'm still puzzled as to why she called you "uncle".

Robert Well, old man—that's exactly what I wanted to tell you. What happened is . . .

Brigit 1 pops back from the kitchen with a tray of clean glasses and her crème de menthe glass

Brigit 1 About this coffee . . .

Robert What about it?

Brigit 1 (*putting the glasses away by the fire*) There isn't any. No beans, that is, only instant. And you won't want that, after all that food and drink, it would only give you wind.

Jacqueline and Brigit 2 enter from the kitchen with drinks

Jacqueline There we are. All done! (*She sits*)

Bernard Already?

Robert You were frightfully fast!

Jacqueline Not me—praise Brigit here. She's terribly dexterous.

Brigit 2 Well, you know how I loathe anything to do with the kitchen— so the faster you do the work, the quicker you can get out of it.

Brigit 1 (*sitting*) And as you've run out of the beans and you're not getting instant, then we don't have to look at the kitchen again.

Brigit 2 That's fine by me. (*She sits*)

Bernard Then everything's fine for everybody. (*Looking at Brigit 2*) So nobody need worry about a thing.

Robert (*looking at Jacqueline*) No— not a thing. Nothing to worry about at all.

Brigit 1 Good. So are we going to dance?

Brigit 2 Dance! That would be marvellous. I adore dancing.

Robert It's rather close—a little sticky . . .

Jacqueline It would be fun. And Brigit does adore it so . . .

Bernard And after all, she elected to dine with us, and now if we're going to dance—because she adores dancing.

Jacqueline Then there's no problem. (*To Robert*) How about you, Robert?

Robert Me? Dancing—well, I really don't mind one way or the other.

Bernard So hands up those who want to dance.

Brigit 1 (*putting her hand up*) Me, please.

Brigit 2 (*putting her hand up*) Me too.

Bernard (*putting his hand up*) And me, makes three. (*To Robert*) And you?

Robert Me?

Bernard Yes, you!

Robert How about you, Jacqueline?

Jacqueline Oh, if you're going to dance, then so will I. (*She puts her hand up*)

Robert All right then. (*He too, raises his hand*) Let's dance.

Bernard There we are. The ayes have it. (*To Robert*) Don't wave the music about—put it on the record-player.

Robert That's just what I was going to do when . . . Oh, well, never mind.

Bernard turns out the main lights. Robert moves up to the record player. Brigit 2 glides towards Bernard but then suddenly turns away. She smiles— teasingly. Bernard finds himself face to face with Jacqueline. The music begins

Bernard (*to Jacqueline*) Shall we . . .?

Jacqueline (*looking at Robert*) Yes. Why not? But maybe—as we're married and the hosts and all that—shouldn't we split up and dance with somebody else?

Brigit 1 (*to Robert*) How about you, Uncle? Going to ask me, are you?

Robert (*to Brigit 1*) Certainly, Brigit.

Brigit 1 Go on then.

Robert On what?

Brigit 1 Ask me!

Robert Oh, very well. Would you like to dance, Brigit?

Brigit 1 Thanks ever so much. I'd love to.

The two couples dance.

Brigit 1 (*to Robert*) Do you come here often, then?

Jacqueline (*to Bernard*) No—it's the very first time.

Robert I have to be careful—I live with my mother and father, you see——

Bernard And if I'm not home by ten o'clock——

Brigit 1 They'll murder me. (*She shrieks with laughter*)

Brigit 2 (*quoting languidly*) "I am as lonely as a goldfish in an empty bowl as old and remote as the moon . . ."

Robert Speaking of fish I thought the whole dinner was perfect.

Jacqueline Oh, they do things very well here——

Brigit 1 Just like at the Academy Ball.

Bernard Where's that?

Brigit 2 "On the moon—the inconstant moon . . ."

Jacqueline That's odd—I didn't think there was anything to paint on the moon.

Brigit 1 Oh! Lots of things have changed since your time, dear.

Robert Whatever—I'm sure we're much better off here than on the moon.

Bernard Why?

Jacqueline We have a comfortable house with lots of cosy bedrooms.

Brigit 1 Just like a hotel.

Brigit 2 Where one sleeps alone—like the goldfish . . .

Bernard Anything can be arranged—all you have to do is ring for room service.

Brigit 1 I think I'll just help myself. I've got a terrible thirst.

Robert It's the heat.

Brigit 1 Which way's the bar? (*She abandons Robert*)

Jacqueline (*leaving Bernard and pouring Brigit 1 a drink*) No, no, no, you must let me do that After all, I'm the mistress of the house.

Bernard advances on Brigit 2 who, in turn, avoids him and moves towards Robert

And you—(*to Brigit 1*)—why don't you dance with Bernard? You'd like that, wouldn't you, Bernard?

Bernard is about to take Brigit 2's hand—but she turns away and takes Robert's hand

Bernard A great pleasure.

Brigit 2 (*to Robert*) Shall we?

Brigit 1 (*to Jacqueline*) I don't want to deprive you of your hubby . . .

Jacqueline (*pouring herself a drink*) Not to worry—I'm sure he's longing to dance with you.

Brigit 1 You think so? (*She drinks her drink*)

Jacqueline I'm positive—just as you're longing to dance with him.

Brigit 1 If you say so, madam. (*She claps her hands*) All right everybody. Change partners!

Jacqueline My turn to play gooseberry. (*She sits*)

Brigit 1 (*in Bernard's arms*) Oooh! You are tall!

Bernard Am I?

Jacqueline Who was it said, "The taller they are, the less trustworthy they are"?

Brigit 1 Whoever said it—it wasn't a midget like me.

Jacqueline Midget Brigit! (*She shrieks with laughter*) Divine!

Brigit 2 (*in the arms of Robert*) Actually—I haven't lived with my mother and father for years.

Robert You haven't?

Brigit 2 No. I'm a big girl now. I can stay out for as long as I like.

Robert Ah! . . . Good.

Brigit 2 And if I choose to, I don't have to go home at all.

Robert Ah! . . . Good.

Brigit 2 I'm completely free. Independent. Liberated.

Robert Ah! . . . Good.

Brigit 1 And I'm just wild about long, tall men.

Jacqueline Doesn't anybody know who said, "The taller they are, the nastier they are"?

Brigit 1 It's really funny, you know—but when I'm dancing with you, I seem even littler than usual.

Bernard I think you exaggerate. (*Losing her momentarily*) Where have you gone?

Brigit 1 I'm still down here . . .

Jacqueline (*rising suddenly*) All right. That's enough! Everybody change partners! (*She puts down her glass and pulls Brigit 1 away from Bernard*)

Robert lets go of Brigit 2

Brigit 1 Are we off again? All change for another shuffle round the track?

Bernard once more heads towards Brigit 2, but she, in order to avoid him, turns to Brigit 1

Brigit 2 (*to Brigit 1*) My turn, I think.

Jacqueline takes hold of Robert, Brigit 1 and Brigit 2 dance

Jacqueline Shall we dance?

Robert My pleasure.

Brigit 1 (*to Brigit 2*) Oooh! You are tall!

Brigit 2 It's these heels.

Jacqueline (*to Robert*) Do you come here often?

Brigit 1 Only when the fleet's in. (*To Brigit 2*) Hello Sailor! (*She shrieks again*)

Bernard, perplexed, pours himself a whisky

Jacqueline (*in Robert's arms*) Are you married?
Robert I don't think so. That is—actually—no.
Jacqueline I knew it! I have this gift, you see . . .
Brigit 2 You lead marvellously.
Brigit 1 Fancy! And I thought you were doing the leading.
Jacqueline And what about me? Can you guess?
Robert Married?
Jacqueline You cheated! You saw my wedding ring.
Robert Where is he?
Jacqueline My husband?
Robert Yes.
Jacqueline Over there with a drink—he's an alcoholic!
Robert Bernard? An alcoholic? No—he hardly drinks at all.
Jacqueline How do *you* know?
Bernard He knows everything. He's my best friend. So we've got to look after him.
Jacqueline What does that mean?
Bernard And when you were clearing the table, he said to me . . . What was it you said to me, old man? That you—that you . . .
Robert That I—that I—I don't remember.
Bernard You must remember. You were yawning at the time.
Robert Oh yes, that's right! I'm frightfully tired—worn out . . .
Bernard Yes, you look terrible, old chap. Positively haggard. I think you ought to get yourself tucked up in bed as soon as possible.
Jacqueline But that's not fair! If Robert goes to bed, then we three girls will have only one man to dance with.
Brigit 1 "Turkish delight", as my mother used to say.
Bernard Yes, dear—so you've said before. (*He turns off the music and switches on the main lights*)

The dancing stops

We can always dance tomorrow. Some other time. Just look at him, he's asleep on his feet.
Robert No need to exaggerate.
Bernard He's past the point of no return. One little push and he'd fall over. (*He pushes Robert on to the sofa*) No. I really think it's time he went to bed.
Brigit That's fine by me, nothing I'd like more than to get my feet up. Can't wait to get myself nice and snug in that great bed. Night, night everybody. (*She moves to the bedroom up* L) Sleep tight. It's not haunted, is it?
Jacqueline What?
Brigit 1 My room? This house?
Jacqueline Not as far as I know.
Bernard Not yet.
Brigit 1 Well, I'll say my prayers anyway. You never know. Better safe than sorry—that's what my mother always used to say!

Brigit 1 exits to the bedroom up L

Brigit 2 Not much more for anyone else to say, is there? Except to wish everybody a very good night.

Bernard So nice of you to come . . .

Jacqueline The agency sent her.

Bernard I just said that because . . .

Robert Because he wanted her to feel part of the family—at home.

Brigit 2 Oh, I *do* feel at home—really loved. If only the party could go on, and on, and on . . .

Brigit 2 glides away into the kitchen

Jacqueline Too much champagne!

Bernard No. It never affects her—only makes her mischievous.

Jacqueline How do *you* know?

Bernard She told Robert—didn't she, Robert?

Robert Something like that.

Bernard While they were dancing together.

Jacqueline When did Robert tell you?

Robert While we were dancing together.

Jacqueline You didn't dance with Bernard.

Robert Didn't I? I danced with everyone else!

Bernard Now don't pick on Robert. (*Moving to the bedroom down* R) You can see the poor chap's exhausted. Go to bed, old man.

Robert I think I will.

Bernard Sleep well.

Robert Oh, I will. No doubt about that. Like a top.

Bernard (*to Jacqueline*) Are you coming?

Jacqueline In a minute, darling—just one or two things to tidy away,

Bernard exits down R

Jacqueline seizes Robert

At last—just you and me.

Robert You wanted to say something?

Jacqueline Come on. Please. It was difficult enough having to sit through dinner—simply bursting to speak. And as for the dancing . . .

Robert I know what you mean. Especially the dancing . . .

Jacqueline How could you know what I mean? You don't suffer. You're not a woman. And if I was a woman worthy of the name . . .

Robert For God's sake keep calm! It's terribly bad to get all worked up in this heat, and after all that food—I was reading about it the other day. When you get over-excited after a heavy meal your intestines turn bright pink!

Jacqueline Considering all I've had to put up with, I should think mine are deep vermilion by now.

Robert You must keep calm.

Jacqueline Why should I be calm when I've just learnt that my husband has been deceiving me—that he's as big a liar and a cheat as you are.

Robert But no more than you are . . .

Jacqueline Thank you. Thank you very much. That's very nice. How dare you call me a cheat?

Robert Well, you are a cheat—or maybe you've confessed to your husband about you and me. Well, have you?

Jacqueline Certainly not.

Robert Then you're a cheat. You're a liar—just like him. Like me. Like my niece. In fact, like the whole world!

Jacqueline Except the new maid.

Robert Well, I expect even the new maid lies now and again—in her fashion.

Jacqueline But she's on her own. She's liberated . . . I wish to God I was.

Robert Darling . . .

Jacqueline Robert . . .

They move to embrace each other

   Bernard enters

Bernard Oh! Still here, are you?

Robert I was just going to bed—just saying good night to Jacqueline.

Jacqueline I was just saying good night to Robert.

Bernard Sleep well, old man.

Robert You too——

Bernard I hope so—but just now, in there, I realized I wasn't a bit sleepy. Must be the heat—but I could really do with a breath of air.

Jacqueline You're going out?

Bernard Yes. But that doesn't mean that you can't go to bed, darling. You don't have to wait up for me.

Jacqueline How long are you going to be?

Bernard I don't know. I'll just go round the garden a couple of times, and maybe down to the bottom of the lane.

Jacqueline Very well, but do remember to slam the front door behind you —otherwise it won't shut properly.

Bernard I know.

Jacqueline I don't want it to stay open all night.

Bernard I'll make sure. (*He goes and opens the front door*)

Jacqueline I'm very nervous about burglars. So I like to hear the door slam. Then I know it's properly shut.

Bernard Don't worry. I'll make certain.

Jacqueline Good night then, Robert.

Robert Good night. And thank you for an enchanted evening.

Jacqueline You're very welcome—an old friend like you.

   Jacqueline exits down R

Bernard (*shutting the front door*) Where are you going?

Robert To bed. That's what you wanted me to do, didn't you?

Bernard That was just to get everybody else to bed. But now they're all safely out of the way, you must stay here while I go and visit Brigit.

Robert Which Brigit?
Bernard My Brigit.
Robert Why must I stay here?
Bernard To keep a look-out. So that you can tip me the wink if there's any danger while I'm with her.
Robert How do I tip you the wink?
Bernard Cough.
Robert You won't hear it through there.
Bernard Whistle then—or sing.
Robert Sing what?
Bernard Doesn't matter what. What do you know?
Robert I don't know anything any more.
Bernard Then whatever comes into your head first—the tune is immaterial. I'm very broad-minded—musically.
Robert Seems to me you're pretty broad-minded in all departments!

Bernard opens the front door

Off round the garden, are you?
Bernard I'm not off anywhere. But I told Jacqueline that I might be going down the lane. All right, then, here I go. (*He slams the door*)
Robert You're immoral—totally immoral!
Bernard Don't be old-fashioned. I'm just going to tell my Brigit to get ready to change rooms with the other one.

Bernard hurries off to the kitchen. Jacqueline enters

Jacqueline What are you doing?
Robert I'm not doing anything. I thought I heard a door slam.
Jacqueline Yes, Bernard's gone to get some air. Isn't that convenient!

Jacqueline goes to embrace him. He points to the bedroom up L

Robert Wonderful! But my niece is in there.
Jacqueline I don't care. She's his mistress. So I don't give a damn if she discovers that you're my lover.

Robert starts to cough

(*Louder*) I don't care, do you hear? I've had a couple of drinks and now I don't give a damn. I want our love to be recognized—recognized and applauded!

Robert coughs again

Why are you coughing?
Robert It must be my hay fever—and the heat . . .
Jacqueline (*louder still*) I want everybody to know that I'm proud to be your mistress!
Robert (*singing*) "There's an old mill by the stream—Nellie Dean . . ."
Jacqueline Why have you started to sing?
Robert In order to stop coughing.
Jacqueline (*louder*) I love you! I'm not ashamed of it! I love you and want you!

Robert (*louder*) "Where we used to sit and dream—Nellie Dean . . ."
Jacqueline (*still louder*) I'm fed up with all the lies and all the cheating!
I want everything out in the open!
Robert (*still louder*) "And the waters as they go—seem to murmur soft
and low . . ."
Jacqueline (*shouting*) I just want to see that woman's face when she learns
that her Uncle Robert is *my* Robert—my lion!
Robert (*crescendo*) "You're my heart's desire—I love you . . ."

Brigit 1 enters from her bedroom

Robert ⎱ "Nellie Dean—Sweet Nellie Dean!" ⎰ (*Singing together in*
Brigit 1 ⎰   ⎱ *harmony*)

*Bernard enters through the front door. He has dust marks on the knees of
his trousers*

Bernard What on earth is going on? Have you both gone mad?
Robert No. We were just feeling nostalgic.
Brigit 1 How about "Let the Rest of the World Go By"?
Brigit 1 ⎱ "With someone like you, I could . . ." ⎰ (*Singing together*)
Robert ⎰
Jacqueline Not just at the moment . . .
Bernard (*to Jacqueline*) Did they wake you up?
Jacqueline No. I was only just going to bed.
Bernard (*to Robert*) And how about you?
Robert Yes, just on my way.
Brigit 1 Well—if you feel like giving "Shine on Harvest Moon" a whirl,
then you know where to find me.

Brigit 1 exits to her bedroom

Jacqueline (*to Bernard*) Are you coming, Bernard?
Bernard Not yet, darling. I came running back because I heard all that
noise. Didn't even get once round the garden.
Jacqueline Off you go then. And don't forget to slam the door behind you.
Bernard I won't forget.

Jacqueline exits to her bedroom

Bernard, limping, advances on Robert

Robert What's up with you?
Bernard As soon as I heard you, I jumped out of the kitchen window. I
must have fallen six feet—on to the crazy paving.
Robert You should dig it up and make it a herbaceous border—lots of
nice soft plants, like African marigolds and hydrangea, very good for
landing on.
Bernard I don't intend to make a habit of leaping out of the window every
time you start to sing!
Robert You told me to sing—I sang.
Bernard What was the trouble?

Robert Well—Jacqueline wanted to go and see if the new maid needed anything.

Bernard I see. Well, in that case, you did very well. Thank you. Now listen—I'm just going to tell the other Brigit to stand by to get ready to change rooms with my Brigit. And while I'm about it, I'm going to tell her to go easy on the coloratura.

Robert Be careful. I'm sure there will be an additional charge for whatever you do.

Bernard I know the score. I've got the money on me. Don't worry.

Bernard exits to Brigit 1's bedroom. Brigit 2 enters from the kitchen. She wears a nightdress

Brigit 2 Where's he gone?

Robert He's in there with the new maid—the real new maid.

Brigit 2 Is that why he jumped out of the kitchen window?

Robert Ah, no. He jumped because he didn't want Jacqueline to find him in there. (*He points to the kitchen*)

Brigit 2 I'm sure he didn't want his wife to find him through there—with me. (*She advances on Robert and puts her hands on his shoulders*) Would you do me a great favour?

Robert If I can. What do you want me to do?

Brigit 2 I want you to kiss me—in front of Bernard. (*She twines her arms round Robert's neck*)

Robert I couldn't do a thing like that.

Brigit 2 Why not?

Robert He's my oldest friend.

Brigit 2 I don't care—you've got to help me. He's been very casual with me. I don't like that. No girl should be kept waiting, and no girl should be asked to do impersonations—I hate having to pretend to be a maid. I think it's time he showed some consideration and paid me some real attention. I want to rouse him—make him jealous!

Robert But what can I do?

Brigit 2 Just pretend. Nothing difficult. Just like this. (*She kisses him*) You see—nothing too complicated.

Robert I think it's very complicated.

Brigit 2 Why? Do you find it so difficult?

Robert Not in the least difficult. On the contrary—it's rather—rather . . .

Brigit Then why won't you help me?

Robert Because your Bernard is my oldest friend.

Brigit 2 You said that already.

Robert And my best friend . . .

Brigit 2 Oh, I understand all that, but I'm an even closer friend of his—in a manner of speaking—and that gives you and me a sort of special relationship . . .

Robert Oh, I can see that—definitely.

Brigit 2 Then because we're all such good friends, you must help me.

Robert Well, I'd like to—really I would, but I'm not very good at all this sort of thing. I've always led a very sheltered life.

Brigit 2 (*leading him to the sofa*) There are times when one must make
sacrifices for one's friends. (*She sits, and draws him down beside her*)

Robert Oh, I'm sure you're right. I'm all for sacrifices. What was it you
wanted me to do again?

Brigit 2 Kiss me.

Robert To make Bernard jealous?

Brigit 2 To make him aware.

Robert Well, there's not much point in me kissing you if he's not here.

Brigit 2 But we ought to practise—so that we're ready when he comes
back, so we can make it look convincing.

Robert Yes—I suppose that makes sense.

Brigit 2 Come on, then. Kiss me. (*She closes her eyes and leans to him*)

Robert leans to kiss her, but does not

Robert Yes, but just kissing you isn't suddenly going to turn him green
with jealousy. After all, he's a man of the world—he's in insurance.

Brigit 2 Well, how should we go about it? What do you suggest?

Robert (*rising and moving away*) Should we try it in a chair?

Brigit 2 Anywhere you like. (*She rises*)

Robert I think it'll be more convincing in a chair—more natural. Here,
sit down over here.

*Brigit 2 goes and sits in a chair, leans back and closes her eyes. She waits
while Robert prowls round behind her*

Brigit 2 So what happens now?

Robert There's an old mill—no that's not right. We must make it look
realistic. It might be better if *I* sat in the chair.

Brigit 2 Just as you like.

*They change places. Robert shuts his eyes and leans back. Brigit 2 leans over
him and kisses him*

Brigit 2 Is that more convincing?

Robert Well, I'm convinced. Do it again.

Brigit 2 Over here. On the sofa.

*She pulls Robert to the sofa. He sits at one end. She lies on it with her head
in his lap*

That should do the trick.

Robert Much more like it. (*He puts a cushion underneath her head, lifting
her head then laying it down on the cushion. He rests his arms on her head,
realizes what he is doing, and raises them again*) We may have some time
to wait before he gets back. You might as well be comfortable.

Brigit 2 I think we should go on practising.

Robert If you insist. (*He takes a deep breath, then leans down and kisses her*)

Brigit 2 That was really rather good. I enjoyed that.

Robert (*breathlessly*) So did I. Awfully nice . . .

Brigit 2 *You* don't look very comfortable.

Robert I'm not very comfortable. It's the heat. I mean, I'm sitting here
with you and a cushion, and it's suddenly terribly close—sticky!

Brigit 2 I hadn't noticed.

Robert Yes, but you're not wearing—that is, you look frightfully cool. That is, there's not much of it, is there? The nightdress. But I'm all buttoned up and starched, and all that sort of thing.

Brigit 2 Well, why don't you let a bit of air in?

Robert What do you mean?

Brigit 2 (*sitting up*) Unbutton a little—here, I'll do it for you. (*She unbuttons his shirt*) Isn't that much better?

Robert Much better. Much cooler.

Brigit 2 So shall we try it again?

Robert One more time?

Brigit 2 It must look convincing.

Robert I'll do my best. (*He kisses her*)

Brigit 2 Wow! I felt that all the way down. You're really good, you know.

Robert Am I?

Brigit 2 Bernard will be furious.

Robert Who's Bernard?

Brigit 2 Who cares? Kiss me again.

Robert I remember. He's my best friend.

Brigit 2 Then he'll understand.

Robert Of course he will.

She pulls his head down. They kiss

Jacqueline enters from her bedroom

Robert and Brigit 2 fall off the sofa—on all fours

Jacqueline What—what on earth are you up to?

Robert Oh, it's you! Hello!

Jacqueline What do you imagine you're doing?

Robert I'm on the floor.

Jacqueline I can see that.

Robert Looking . . . Lost my cuff-stud—the thingamejig—what-do-you-call-it—collar-link . . . Cuff-link—that's it! Lost my cuff-link—looking for it. Brigit's helping me. Aren't you, Brigit. Look for it, Brigit!

At this moment Bernard enters—followed by Brigit 1

Jacqueline Well, well, well. That's how it is, eh?

Bernard How what is?

Jacqueline I thought you were out for a walk round the garden.

Bernard There's going to be a storm.

Jacqueline But it hasn't started raining yet.

Bernard No. But I thought it would be a good idea to have a word with Brigit here—to ask her if she'd mind *not* singing again in case it stopped you going to sleep—*before* I went out.

Jacqueline So you had a little wander round *her* room?

Bernard I was in her room . . .

Jacqueline (*to Robert*) What do you say to that, Uncle Robert?

Bernard Uncle?

Jacqueline *Her* uncle . . .
Bernard (*to Brigit 1*) You're *his* niece?
Brigit 1 She's just told you so.
Bernard (*to Robert*) She's your niece?
Robert She just said so.
Bernard Is that why she called you uncle?
Robert A good a reason as any.
Bernard I can't believe . . . I think you're pulling my leg.
Jacqueline Not at all.
Bernard She can't be his niece. He can't be her uncle because . . .
Brigit 2 I'm the new maid.
Jacqueline Yes, dear—we know that, dear.
Brigit 1 So that makes me the niece!
Jacqueline And I can prove it!
Bernard What proof? Where did you get it?
Jacqueline From Robert.
Bernard Robert?
Jacqueline Yes! And I also have proof—*written* proof—that she's *your* mistress!
Bernard Jacqueline! Really! How on earth can she be my mistress when you know perfectly well that she's Robert's mistress?
Jacqueline That's very nice! Are you really trying to insinuate that he's in love with his niece?
Bernard No. Not at all. Wouldn't dream of it! I'm simply telling you that she can't be his niece because . . .
Brigit 2 I'm the new maid!
Jacqueline You don't have to keep on reminding us! We know already!
Brigit 2 Good!
Bernard Darling! You've got it all wrong . . .
Jacqueline I've *seen* the proof.
Bernard The proof of what?
Jacqueline That she's your mistress. I've *seen* it.
Bernard (*to Robert*) Have *you* seen it?
Robert I have.
Bernard Am I going mad?
Jacqueline Tell him, Robert. You tell him if he won't believe *me*!
Bernard Yes—you tell me, old man . . .
Robert All right. It so happened that—as I was coming to visit you—I brought my niece along—didn't I, Brigit?
Brigit 1 No doubt about it!
Jacqueline Go on. Hurry up—tell him what happened next!
Robert I tried to get Jacqueline to believe that Brigit was *my* mistress—so that she wouldn't start suspecting that she was *yours*!
Jacqueline You see!
Bernard Mine?
Robert Yes.
Bernard My mistress?
Robert Yes.

Bernard (*pointing to Brigit 1*) That!

Robert Yes.

Bernard Wonderful! I'm not going mad; I *am* mad!

Brigit 1 And I'm very broad-minded myself. I think it's time that I put my cards on the table.

Brigit 2 Are you planning to take my place?

Brigit 1 You took mine!

Brigit 2 So it's my turn to be Mister Bernard's mistress?

Bernard Not now, Brigit. Both Brigits. This is no time . . .

Brigit 2 Darling Bernard! I was waiting for you—longingly—in my lonely room; all ready and desperate! (*She puts her arms round Bernard's neck*)

Bernard Thank you. Very amusing.

Robert Amusing.

Jacqueline Very.

Brigit 2 I couldn't understand why you stayed away so long.

Bernard (*trying to push her away*) That's enough, Brigit. I know it's your birthday and you're over-excited, but that's enough. Laughter before eleven, tears before seven . . .

Brigit 2 But I'm longing to be alone with you, to hold you close—just the two of us . . .

Robert (*taking Brigit 2's arms off Bernard*) Stop it, Brigit. It's far too hot for all that!

Jacqueline Quite. Perhaps you had a fraction too much to drink, my dear. Well, you've been frightfully witty but now it's time for you to remember your place. You can go to your room now.

Brigit 2 Go to my room?

Jacqueline At once, please. We have things to talk about—private matters —which were best discussed among those concerned and *not* in front of the domestic staff.

Brigit 2 Very well. I will go to my room.

Jacqueline Thank you, Brigit.

Brigit 2 But if I can be of any help to anyone looking for a mistress— don't hesitate to call me.

Jacqueline That's sweet of you—but we already have one.

Brigit 2 Do you seriously think she's up to it?

Jacqueline That's none of your business. Just kindly take yourself to bed.

Brigit 2 Don't worry. I'm going.

Brigit 2 exits to the kitchen

Brigit 1 tries to creep away

Brigit 1 If it's all the same to you. It *has* been a long day. I think I'll hop into bed now . . .

Jacqueline catches hold of her

Jacqueline Oh, no. You're not slipping away—you're very much the *point* of the discussion. I know all about you. All about you and my husband!

Brigit 1 Then you must have quite an imagination, madam.

Jacqueline And intelligence. I'm not a little middle-class nobody—I'm a sophisticated, modern woman. And I think its splendid that we four are all together like this. It is time for the truth, the whole truth. Let's all be honest with each other.

Bernard Jacqueline . . .

Jacqueline All of us! And I'll begin if you like—it's my turn! I'd like to introduce *my* lover!

Brigit 1 Fancy—Uncle Bob!

Robert Jacqueline! Bernard—stop her! She's not herself. Your wife's not well!

Jacqueline I've never felt better! Well, Bernard—what do you say?

Bernard To the news? That you're Robert's mistress?

Robert Now look here . . .

Jacqueline You be quiet, Robert. Let Bernard answer.

Bernard All I can say is—that it's not exactly news to me.

Brigit 1 It isn't?

Bernard No. I've known for some time.

Jacqueline About Robert and me?

Bernard Yes—and you see I sympathized; I understood the attraction—he's a very charming and decent young man.

Brigit 1 Oh, yes. Yes, you're right enough there—a very nice gentleman.

Robert Please . . .

Jacqueline How long have you known?

Bernard Since it began.

Jacqueline No!

Brigit 1 And you never said nothing?

Robert Be quiet. (*To Bernard*) You, that it had to be you. My oldest friend. To deceive *you*!

Brigit 1 But you didn't deceive him. He knew all about it.

Robert Be quiet.

Bernard But she's right. I knew. And because I love you both, I didn't say anything. I didn't want to interrupt your happiness.

Robert A rat!

Brigit 1 (*kneeling on the stool*) Where?

Robert Be quiet. Beside you . . .

Brigit 1 I don't see anything . . .

Robert (*to her*) Be quiet. (*To Bernard*) Beside you, I'm a rat!

Bernard No, old man . . .

Robert Yes, I am, old man—a rat who you took for a friend.

Bernard (*taking his hand*) But you *are* my friend.

Robert I don't know what to say—I'm deeply ashamed.

Bernard Nonsense . . .

Jacqueline But weren't you jealous?

Brigit 1 Why should he be jealous? A fine, upstanding gentleman like him? He don't have to be jealous of anyone: not of a rat anyway.

Robert (*to Brigit 1*) If you don't keep quiet, I'm going to strangle you!

Bernard But she's right. I wasn't jealous because I adore my wife—the only thing that matters is *her* happiness.

Brigit 1 Isn't he lovely!

Bernard All I ask is that you conduct your—your liaison—with dignity. And perhaps you should avoid too many martinis in the Hilton Bar. Lots of my colleagues go there—people in the insurance business— they see you together, and they *will* gossip.

Brigit 1 I think you're being very reasonable.

Robert Be quiet!

Bernard And as I've already told you—my happiness depends solely on yours. So love one another—be happy!

Brigit 1 That's beautiful—really sad.

Bernard I haven't finished yet.

Brigit 1 Beg your pardon.

Bernard Be happy. That's all I desire. (*He moves towards the front door*)

Brigit 1 Lovely. (*To Jacqueline*) I'll tell you what, madam. Your hubby is as big on the inside as he is on the outside. What a smashing bloke!

Jacqueline Yes—extraordinary. (*To Bernard*) But are you going out again?

Bernard Yes.

Jacqueline You're not going to stay with her? (*She indicates Brigit 1*)

Bernard Not tonight. I don't think it would be proper. I have to get used to the idea that you now know all about me and Brigit—about Brigit and I . . .

Jacqueline I see—you and Brigit. Yes . . .

Bernard I *was* going to tell you. I was working myself up to it, but I didn't know *how* to tell you. That you've discovered is something of a shock to me. That's why I must take a walk in the night air—to reflect. (*He limps to the front door and opens it*)

Jacqueline But you're limping!

Bernard It's nothing. It'll wear off if I can only manage to get myself to the end of the lane. Don't trouble yourselves about me. You and Robert—well, you two do as you feel you must do. Only one thing, old man . . .

Robert Yes?

Bernard When you go to bed—remember to switch off the lights.

Bernard exits through the front door

Brigit 1 A lovely fellah!

Robert A real friend! A saint!

Brigit 1 A Pope!

Jacqueline No need to exaggerate. The man's not so stainless as all that! I think you've overlooked the fact that he keeps a mistress—keeps *you*!

Brigit 1 That's true; very true. But he was very kind about you two. The one sort of cancels out the other.

Robert He forgave us.

Jacqueline He had to! He's just as guilty as we are!

Brigit 1 Well, I happen to like him. So I'm going to bed now, dear. Don't mind me calling you "dear" do you, madam? After all, if your bloke's my uncle and my bloke's your husband, then we're practically related— sort of half-sisters. Funny, eh? And I've never seen you till this after- noon! Then it's a rum old world. . . .

Robert As your mother used to say.
Brigit 1 I didn't know you knew my mother.

Brigit 1 exits to the bedroom up L

Jacqueline There! Everything out in the open at last! We don't have to worry about a thing any more. And the night is young!
Robert Maybe—but I'm sure Bernard isn't quite so calm as he sounded. He's out there somewhere—watching us!
Jacqueline I don't care! (*She tries to hold him*)
Robert No. Please—Jacqueline. Let go!
Jacqueline He wants us to be happy! That's what he said. I can only be happy with you—and in there! Your room! (*She points to the bedroom down L, then tries to pull him towards the door*)
Robert All right—in a minute. I must just pop into the bathroom—clean my teeth—all that sort of thing.
Jacqueline But you will hurry, darling? (*She blows him a kiss*)
Robert As fast as I can—darling. (*He blows her a kiss*)

Jacqueline exits to the bedroom down L

Robert moves towards the bathroom

Brigit 2 enters from the kitchen

Brigit 2 I'm still waiting!
Robert I'm sure he won't be long. He's in the garden.
Brigit 2 I don't care where he is; I'm not waiting for him.
Robert You're not?
Brigit 2 No. It's *you* I want.
Robert I beg your pardon?
Brigit 2 You. We were just getting somewhere last time when that woman came in. I don't want to be interrupted again—let's go into your room.

Robert steps between Brigit 2 and the bedroom door

Robert Oh, no. No, no. Not now!
Brigit 2 Why not?
Robert Not very prudent.
Brigit 2 Why not?
Robert Because . . . Think about it! If he doesn't find you in there—(*Indicating the kitchen*)—he's going to come and wake me up to tell me that he's lost you! Can't find you!
Brigit 2 So what?
Robert So if you're in there—(*Indicating the bedroom down L*)—he's going to find us, isn't he? Together.
Brigit 2 So what?
Robert So what—"so what"? Don't you understand?
Brigit 2 Of course, I understand. I understand perfectly that you're much more nervous about Jacqueline than you are about me—because she's waiting for you—in there! (*She points to the bedroom down L*)
Robert Jacqueline? In there? You're not serious.

At this moment, Jacqueline enters from the bedroom down L—*knocking Robert into the arm of Brigit 2*

Jacqueline Robert, where are you? What are you doing?
Robert (*going into a tango pose*) Demonstrating. She's teaching me to tango.
Jacqueline This is hardly the moment for a tango lesson!
Brigit 2 I didn't realize, madam, that that was *your* bedroom.
Jacqueline My bedroom? No, of course, it's not my bedroom. (*She crosses to the door down* R) I sleep in here. I was in *there* just to see that Mister Robert had everything he needed. And as everything *is* there, then Mister Robert can safely go to bed.
Robert Thank you so much.
Jacqueline And as you're so patently in need of sleep, I suggest you get into bed as soon as possible.
Robert I'm on my way.
Brigit 2 Me too. Good night, madam.
Jacqueline Good night.
Brigit 2 And thank you for everything. (*She moves to the bedroom door down* L)
Jacqueline Where are you going?
Brigit 2 I'm not sure—I'm confused—I think it's this way. (*She moves towards the kitchen*)
Jacqueline That's better.
Robert I'll just brush the teeth—won't be long. (*He moves towards the bathroom*)
Jacqueline No. Do hurry.

Jacqueline exits to her bedroom down R

Immediately, Brigit 2 and Robert turn away from their respective doors. They move towards each other quickly. They kiss

Brigit 1 enters from the bedroom up L

Brigit 1 Aha!
Robert What is it now? What are you up to?
Brigit 1 I'm not up to anything. You're the one who's up to something, Uncle Bob. Hanky-panky, if you ask me.
Robert What do you want?
Brigit 1 It's not what I want, it's what Mister Bernard wants—he wants us to swop and me to sleep in the bedroom by the kitchen.
Brigit 2 Yes. It was all worked out—all agreed.
Brigit 1 So, if you're still up to it, dear . . .
Brigit 2 Sure. Why not? It's all the same to me. (*She moves to the bedroom up* L)
Brigit 1 (*moving to the kitchen*) Right you are, then. (*To Robert*) So you can have which one you like—(*she indicates the two doors*)—I mean, it's not the geography which counts with you, is it?
Robert God! I'm not a violent man, but if you don't keep out of my way I'm going to murder you!

Brigit 1 Steady, it's none of my fault, you know. I'm only passing through. No need to turn nasty. But if that smashing fellah pops back, I'll tell him he'd better take a look in there. (*She points to the bedroom up* L)
Robert You wouldn't be so malicious—spiteful!
Brigit 1 Oh, wouldn't I? It's up to you, Uncle—you know the going rate!

Brigit 1 exits to the kitchen

Brigit 2 Now's our chance. Come on!
Robert What if we get caught?
Brigit 2 Are you a coward?
Robert No. I'm a lion. All right, you're on! I'll just whizz into the bathroom and clean the teeth . . .
Brigit 2 Don't take all night, darling.
Robert I won't, darling.
Brigit 2 I adore you! My King of the Jungle!

Brigit 2 growls, then exits to the bedroom up L

Robert opens the bathroom door, looks back to the bedroom where Brigit 2 has gone, changes his mind, cleans his teeth with his finger, and moves to the bedroom door

Jacqueline enters from her bedroom. She wears a nightdress identical to that of Brigit 2

Jacqueline What are you doing?
Robert Thinking.
Jacqueline About what?
Robert I still don't like it, darling—if he was to find us in there . . . (*He points down* L)
Jacqueline He won't be back for ages—not with that limp!
Robert We can't be certain. It might start to rain at any minute . . .
Jacqueline Then he'll shelter under a tree.
Robert Not in a thunderstorm. Too dangerous—get struck by lightning!
Jacqueline Then we won't go in there—(*pointing down* L)—but in there. (*She points up* L)
Robert But Brigit's in there.
Jacqueline Which Brigit?
Robert My niece.
Jacqueline Very suitable. Instead of his mistress, he'll find *us*. Poetic justice! (*She goes to the bedroom up* L *and knocks*)
Robert No. Listen. Jacqueline, darling . . .

Brigit 2 appears

Jacqueline I hope I'm not disturbing you.
Brigit 2 Not at all.
Jacqueline But you're in Brigit's room!
Brigit 2 I *am* Brigit.
Jacqueline The other Brigit.
Robert How very strange!

Jacqueline What happened?

Brigit 2 I don't remember—in this house though, it's awfully easy to make a mistake, to get lost . . .

Jacqueline Well, never mind—we can always move you somewhere else.

Brigit 2 You can?

Jacqueline Certainly—you can go into this gentleman's room.

Brigit 2 With the gentleman?

Jacqueline No. On your own. He won't be in his room, because he'll be in your room.

Robert If it's going to be a bother . . .

Jacqueline No bother at all—just a simple turn around. You'll be in there—(*she points down* L)—and he'll be in there. (*She points up* L) All right?

Brigit 2 (*moving down* L) Fine—perfectly straight forward. And you'll be in there? (*She points down* R)

Jacqueline (*moving down* R) Exactly! I'll be in here. So that's all sorted out. One moment, though . . .

Brigit 2 What is it?

Jacqueline Your nightdress—it's the same as mine!

Brigit 2 So it is.

Jacqueline Where did you get it?

Brigit 2 I—I can't quite remember . . .

Robert Nightdresses like that—well, you see them everywhere. I had one just like it . . .

Jacqueline Mine was a present from my husband.

Brigit 2 A present from your husband? You too?

Jacqueline What do you mean—you too?

Brigit 2 What a coincidence—so was mine!

Jacqueline A present from my husband?

Robert She meant to say from *her* boy-friend.

Brigit 2 Yes. That's what I meant.

Robert Probably a present for your birthday?

Brigit 2 No—for Valentine's Day.

Jacqueline How sweet! And the dress you were wearing at dinner?

Brigit 2 That was a present for Easter.

Jacqueline Really? Now I begin to understand why you're unhappy working as a maid.

Brigit 2 Right—I'm just hanging on in there—waiting for Christmas!

Brigit 2 exits down L

Jacqueline Now, I know everything!

Robert Everything?

Jacqueline She's been brainwashed—suddenly found religion or something.

Robert Then why isn't she a nun? Why go on slaving as a maid?

Jacqueline Because her lover's wife has just returned unexpectedly from visiting relations in the south so she's got nowhere to sleep! And because of the religious thing, she's riddled with guilt!

Robert I don't think it's anything like that at all.

Jacqueline Whatever—it's all decidedly odd. I've never seen a maid who looks and dresses like that one does. But I'm not a detective—and at the moment I'm only interested in us. At last, everything's in order.

Robert At last—yes—maybe—but it's frightfully late.

Jacqueline (*pulling Robert to the door up* L) But Bernard wants us to be happy. He said so. And he's your friend. He's given us his blessing!

Robert All right—but I must clean my teeth.

Jacqueline Again?

Robert Not again—I was never able to get into the bathroom in the first place.

Jacqueline All right. But do be quick, darling. (*She turns off the main lights*)

Jacqueline blows Robert a kiss and exits to the bedroom up L

Robert As fast as I can, darling. (*He blows her a kiss then turns to the bathroom*)

Bernard enters through the main door

Ah! It's you, old man!

Bernard I thought you'd forgotten the signal.

Robert The signal?

Bernard Couldn't you have switched the light off sooner?

Robert Ah. Difficult. A lot of traffic—a lot going on.

Bernard But you handled it all very smoothly—as you did everything else. Mind you, I thought the "rat" business was going a bit far.

Robert Did you?

Bernard Overdone—for my taste. But otherwise, the whole thing was perfect. (*He switches on the main lights*)

Robert You thought so?

Bernard Absolutely. I knew at once that Jacqueline had persuaded you to go along with that absurd story about you and her having an affair—out of revenge; to get her own back. I knew there wasn't a shred of truth in it. I know my wife too well.

Robert So do I.

Bernard Why was she so angry with me?

Robert Well, you see—she found a stub in your cheque book made out to the Fur Company. She thought you'd bought a mink coat for the maid, the *real* maid.

Bernard And she thought the maid was having an affair with me?

Robert Right—so that's why I had to make up the uncle story.

Bernard Brilliant. You played it all like a champion, old chap. I really do congratulate you. Well done!

Robert Thank you.

Bernard Have the Brigits switched rooms yet?

Robert Yes. But your wife found out.

Bernard No problem. If Jacqueline *knows* that your niece is safe on this side—(*pointing to the kitchen*)—then she won't come looking for me in the maid's room. (*He indicates the bedroom up* L)

Robert Probably not . . .

Bernard So there we are, old man—everything in order at last. Perfect! (*He moves down* R) Thank you for your help.

Robert It was nothing.

Bernard It was invaluable. Well played—really well played! Where's my wife?

Robert gestures wildly

Ah! In the bathroom?

Robert Yes— the bathroom . . . I expect—

Bernard exits down R

Where was I? Ah, yes—bathroom: the teeth. Have to brush the teeth!

Robert exits to the bathroom. As the bathroom door closes, Brigit 2 enters from down L, *crosses and knocks on the kitchen door*

Brigit 1 (*off*) Yes!

Brigit 2 Excuse me . . .

Brigit 1 enters from the kitchen

Brigit 1 What's up now?

Brigit 2 Would you mind frightfully if I slept in there? All my things are still there—all my little, personal things . . .

Brigit 1 And all mine are in mine.

Brigit 2 You'll have to leave them till the morning—now Robert's in there. Look—if you don't mind going in there. (*She indicates the bedroom down* L)

Brigit 1 I don't mind, dear. Not if it's a help. (*She moves to the bedroom down* L)

Brigit 2 Thank you—and by the way—that mink coat . . .

Brigit 1 Yes?

Brigit 2 You can keep it.

Brigit 1 Me? You're giving it to me?

Brigit 2 Easy come, easy go.

Brigit 1 But what am I going to do with it?

Brigit 2 Wear it.

Brigit 1 In this weather?

Brigit 2 Then just hang it in a cupboard—as a souvenir!

Brigit 2 exits to the kitchen

Brigit 1 Well. Thank you. Very kind, I'm sure. Fancy, me in a mink! (*She starts singing as she moves to the door down* L)

Robert enters from the bathroom

Robert Where are you going?

Brigit 1 To my room.

Robert But not in there. That's not your room, that's my—my . . .

Brigit 1 Your little friend's room? Oh, no, Uncle—not any more.

Robert No?

Brigit 1 Afraid not. But if you want to know where she's gone—well, you know the going rate for information.

Robert All too well. I'm going to find my case.

Robert exits to the bedroom down L

Brigit 1 Now where am I? I'd better try the bathroom. I can always sleep in the bath!

Brigit 1 exits to the bathroom. Brigit 2 enters from the kitchen, dressed as when she arrived, carrying her shoes, case and handbag. Robert enters from the bedroom down L, carrying his jacket, hat and case

Brigit 2 Ah! There you are! I thought you were in there. (*She indicates the bedroom up L*)

Robert No. Not for a long time actually—not since you—since you and I . . .

Brigit 2 My darling—do you feel strange?

Robert Lightheaded! Extraordinary!

Brigit 2 Darling! (*She kisses him*) What's happening?

Robert I'm not sure—but I'm not complaining! My car's outside—shall we go?

Brigit 2 Anywhere you like, for as long as you like.

Robert and Brigit 2 hurry to the front door. Robert taps the barometer as he passes

Robert Ah! Seems there isn't going to be a storm after all. Things are looking up! After you, darling.

Brigit 2 exits through the front door. Robert follows, closing it. Then he opens it again, puts his head round, looks round the empty room, and smiles

Mustn't forget to slam the door!

Robert exits and slams the front door behind him. Bernard enters and crosses to the bathroom door, wearing his dressing-gown. Jacqueline, wearing a towelling wrap, enters from the bedroom up L and crosses to the kitchen door

Bernard opens the bathroom door

Brigit 1 enters

Brigit 1 What do you want?

Bernard (*backing*) Excuse me!

Brigit 1 What's up now?

Jacqueline That's what I'd like to know! I heard the door slam . . .

Bernard Where have you been?

Jacqueline In bed.

Bernard I didn't see you.

Jacqueline You didn't look. I was waiting.

Bernard For the bathroom?

Jacqueline For an explanation.

Bernard (*to Brigit 1*) Would you please tell my wife who you are.

Brigit 1 I'm Robert's niece.

Bernard I want the truth. Who are you?

Brigit 1 I'm your mistress!

Bernard The truth, woman! Tell the truth!

Brigit 1 What truth? Where is the truth? It's hard to know what's true and what's false in this house. Come to think of it, it's hard to know where you *are* half the time! I'm not sure, mind you—but maybe I'm the temporary maid. You never know your luck!

Brigit 1 exits to the bedroom up L

Bernard You see, angel—now why on earth should I give that creature a fur coat?

Jacqueline I can't imagine.

Bernard Of course you can't, because I didn't! The cheque was to settle an insurance claim.

Jacqueline If that one's the real maid then, who was the other one?

Bernard Robert's girl-friend.

Jacqueline What? His what?

Bernard His mistress. He was a bit nervous about bringing her down here and—well, I can't remember the details now, but he begged me to help him to get you to believe she was the maid.

Jacqueline The liar! (*She goes to the bedroom down* L *and looks in*)

Bernard I know—but as he's my oldest friend, I couldn't let him down. I just had to go along with it . . .

Jacqueline Robert! He's gone!

Bernard opens the kitchen door and looks in

Bernard Brigit! She's gone, too. They've gone together. You see? What did I tell you?

Jacqueline The long and the short of it is that—out of all of us—you were the only one telling the truth.

Bernard Nearly.

Jacqueline I'm very proud of you. (*She kisses him*)

Bernard Where are we going?

Jacqueline To bed.

Bernard You and I?

Jacqueline Why not? We *are* married—remember?

Jacqueline moves to the bedroom down R

Bernard I remember.

Bernard limps after Jacqueline: they exit together. Brigit 1 enters with her shopping-bag. She wears the mink coat, which is much too long and large for her, and holds a wad of £5 notes

Brigit 1 I'm off. (*She puts the money in a pocket of the coat and finds a card there. She takes it out and reads*) "For Brigit. Happy Birthday, darling." Now, isn't that nice! Specially when it's not my birthday. Still, it's the thought that counts, as my mother used to say. (*She returns the card to the pocket with the money and comes downstage. She looks at herself in the coat—using the "fourth wall" as a long mirror. She speaks out front*) Talk about mutton dressed as lamb! Still, it's not bad, considering I was only temporary—just passing through . . .

Brigit 1 marches off to the front door, singing cheerfully

"There's an old mill by the stream . . .",

as—

the CURTAIN *falls*

FURNITURE AND PROPERTY LIST

ACT I

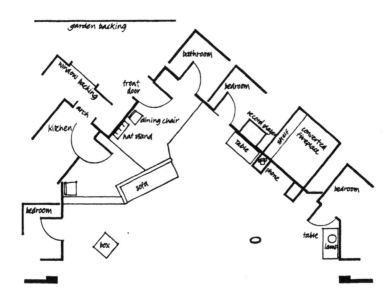

On stage: Box. *On it:* magazine
           2 dining chairs
           Hat stand. *On it:* **Bernard's** driving-gloves, sunglasses
           Folding table (closed). *On it:* Pile of records. *In drawer:* 6 table mats
           Record-player with record on turntable
           Pile of records by fireplace on shelf
           Occasional table. *On it:* ashtray, table lamp
           Stool
           Armchair. *On it:* cushion
           Sofa. *On it:* cushion
           On wall by front door: barometer set to "Rain"
           On fireplace shelf: telephone, pair of candlesticks, bottles of whisky,
               gin, crème de menthe, vodka, vermouth, martini, brandy, port,
               sherry, tonic water, empty bottle of whisky, ice bucket and ice,
               bottle opener, cocktail shaker (liquid preset), glasses, empty vase
           Carpet

Off stage: Hairbrush **(Jacqueline)**
           Suitcase, bunch of roses **(Robert)**
           Door slam (for use of cast)
           Empty shopping-basket, handbag **(Jacqueline)**
           Shopping-basket full of odds and ends **(Brigit 1)**

Full shopping-basket **(Jacqueline)**
Box of groceries **(Bernard)**
Full bottles of gin and whisky, plate of lemons, box of candles
    (Jacqueline)
Apron, duster, teacloth **(Brigit 1)**
Valise, handbag **(Brigit 2)**
Duplicate vase and roses **(Jacqueline)**
Colander of shrimps **(Brigit 1)**
Pile of plates: 4 dinner, 4 dessert, 4 side **(Brigit 1)**
Dining chair **(Jacqueline)**
Tray of cutlery: 4 large knives, 4 large forks, 4 dessert spoons, 4
    dessert forks, 4 butter knives, 2 serving spoons **(Brigit 1)**
4 napkins in rings **(Brigit 2)**
Cheque book **(Jacqueline)**
2 ice buckets with champagne bottles, 1 bottle opened **(Bernard)**
Small tray with pepper and salt **(Brigit 2)**
Tray with 4 large and 4 small wine glasses **(Brigit 1)**
Lobster dish **(Brigit 2)**

Personal: **Robert:** watch, lighter
    Bernard: watch, ring, lighter (in dinner jacket pocket)
    Brigit 1: watch
    Jacqueline: wedding ring, watch
    Brigit 2: mink coat with card in pocket

ACT II

Strike: All props from dinner table
    Cheque book
    Record from record-player
    1 dining chair
    Candles
    All dirty glasses

Set: 2 upright chairs in original positions
    Stool in original position
    Armchair in original position
    Table (closed) in original position
    5 records ready on fireplace shelf
    Telephone in folding table
    Barometer at "Fair"

Check: **Robert's** hat, case and jacket in bedroom down L
    Brigit 1's bag and mink coat in bedroom up L
    Card in pocket of mink coat

LIGHTING PLOT

Property fittings required: pendant, wall brackets, table lamp
Interior: A living-room. The same scene throughout

ACT I	Early evening	
To open:	General effect of early evening daylight	
Cue 1	**Robert:** "I might have guessed." *Slight general fade*	(Page 12)
Cue 2	**Robert:** "How—how much?" *General fade*	(Page 39)
Cue 3	**Robert** and **Bernard** light candles *Bring up lighting over dinner table*	(Page 43)
Cue 4	**All:** "Happy Birthday . . ." *Flash of lightning*	(Page 43)

ACT II	Night	
To open:	All practicals on. Dark outside window	
Cue 5	**Bernard** turns out main lights *Snap off pendant and wall brackets*	(Page 47)
Cue 6	**Bernard** turns on main lights *Snap on pendant and wall brackets*	(Page 50)
Cue 7	**Jacqueline** turns off main lights *Snap off pendant and wall brackets*	(Page 66)
Cue 8	**Bernard** turns on main lights *Snap on pendant and wall brackets*	(Page 66)

EFFECTS PLOT

ACT I

Lightning Source UK Ltd.
Milton Keynes UK
UKHW020013120422
401412UK00006B/622